HEROIC MARYPORT

BY JOHN LITTLE

HEROIC
MARYPORT

1860-1950

JOHN LITTLE

ISBN 9798872470533

Dedicated to the memory of Thomas Q Reay,
sometime Coxswain of the Maryport Lifeboat, twice
winner of the RNLI Bronze Medal for Gallantry in
saving life at sea.

'Then out spake brave Horatius,
The Captain of the Gate:
"To every man upon this earth
Death cometh soon or late.
And how can man die better
Than facing fearful odds,
For the ashes of his fathers,
And the temples of his gods?"'

PREFACE

Maryport in Cumberland, is a quiet town. Much of its old industry has departed, and its docks, once busy with ocean going vessels, are now a haven for small boats, trawlers and yachts. The prosperity associated with being an international port has also gone, and Maryport looks for new ways to develop her community and shape a new vision for the future. It would not appear, at first glance, that there is anything extraordinary about its people, who would probably see themselves as normal average Cumbrians. Perhaps they are, but once upon a time, Maryport was a home for heroes, and some of the things they did were quite astonishing.

One of the greatest virtues that human beings esteem is Courage. It comes in several forms, the most spectacular of which is Valour; the sort of courage that charges an enemy machine gun post, armed only with a rifle. It may also be seen when a person charges into a blazing house to rescue a baby. Then there is bravery, where a man, who can swim, sees another person in the water, in danger of drowning, and without hesitation they leap in to rescue someone who is more helpless in that element than they themselves are. We have other words to describe it, such as bravery, boldness, intrepidity.

Fortitude is the sort of courage where someone can bear the most painful or adverse conditions over an extended period, maybe of hours, or maybe of weeks

1

or months, even years. People often show fortitude in the face of long and debilitating illness.

What constitutes courage is subjective then, but for me, having seen and read so many articles and books over the years, the greatest form of courage appears to be that of the person who knows the risk, shakes and trembles with fear, yet still goes ahead and does what needs to be done at risk of their own life. This is because they have had to overcome their own fears first before they acted.

I decided that I could not possibly include every heroic act in my little book about Maryport heroes; that was too ambitious, especially given the difficulties involved in finding what any particular individual did after the passage of many years. Many people have done brave things that were not recorded. Others went off to war, some were killed, others came home but leave no citations or newspaper articles to relate what they did. The book is based then, on the winning of an award of some sort, a medal, a parchment, or a vellum, or perhaps some mark of esteem like a gold watch or money. There is one exception, which is a feat of endurance so astonishing that I could not leave it out.

Modern media concentrates too much on the negative. I have seen Maryport described too many times as "Scaryport", a convenient rhyme though malicious in effect. Sixty years ago I walked through Maryport with my Grandmother who lived in Grasslot at that time. I little knew that I was rubbing shoulders with heroes. It is my hope that those who read this book, and they will probably only be Maryporters, will feel a sense of pride, and even amazement about the people who came before them.

I wish to thank my wife Ruth, and David Banks of Beechville, Nova Scotia, for proof-reading the book, and to Betty Telford for beta-reading it. Leigh Smith of Maryport I must also thank for his family photo of Coxswain Benn, and for his permission to use an image of Edward Smith VC. his cousin three times removed. Mike Park has supplied me with a photograph of his Grandfather Stanley Roast, who took on the Japanese army under the most perilous conditions imaginable; thank you. I am grateful to Paul Williamson, of Firpress, for the photographs of his grandfather Flight Lieutenant Maurice Williamson. The British Newspaper Archives I also thank, having mined them in depth for months. I hope you, reader, enjoy this little book, and perhaps you will look at your old town with new, and very proud eyes. People may not have risked their lives for the ashes of their fathers and the temples of their gods, but they have stood many times as keepers of the gate - to life and death, faced fearful odds, and come through as heroes and worthy of remembrance. For that reason I have decided that any profits from this book shall go to Maryport Rescue, so that the memory of what has gone before, can in some small way help to save more lives.

Author's comments are in italics. Also in italics are passages where the original article has been paraphrased, either for interest or brevity.

John Little
January 2024

HEROIC MARYPORT

THE 1860s

12 June 1863 Maryport Advertiser
Death of Eleanor Rome

If more carefully chronicled, the annals of the poor furnish many true examples of true heroism and philanthropy. When the rich die, though they have never distinguished themselves beyond anything but a passion for laying up treasures on earth, in violation of the command of their divine master, we have long obituary notices of their worthless lives. A thousand obsequious flatterers are ever ready to write an ostentatious record of their history, and pen their fulsome epitaphs, while the worthy poor often "live neglected, and forgotten, die."

In the death of Eleanor Rome we consider that Maryport has lost a benefactress, for she has long been labouring among her poor neighbours as a voluntary nurse and medical adviser. She has lightened the pain of many a sufferer on a bed of sickness, and cheered them by her presence in the dark hour of death.

As a midwife and doctress among the young children of the poor, her services were invaluable. She was, in fact, the Florence Nightingale of this town, and it would redound to the credit of the inhabitants, if a monument were erected to her memory, in the cemetery, as evincing a proper appreciation of her services, and her worth.

THE 1870s

7 November 1873 Echo (London)

The following cases of remarkable courage have just been brought before the Royal Humane Society... to HPS Black, aged 14, for saving J Henderson who fell into the water at Maryport.

8 May 1875 West Cumberland Times

A fall into the harbour and a narrow escape from drowning were, on Wednesday, sustained by a boy called Robert Sample, about ten years of age. While the boy was playing in front of the Harbour Hotel, he fell into the water, from which he was rescued by a sailor. He was unconscious when rescued and it was not without some trouble that his resuscitation was effected. This, we are informed, was the fourth time that the boy has experienced a similar accident, and a similar rescue.

12 October 1877 Maryport Advertiser
Boy saved from drowning

On Tuesday about noon, some boys were playing on the North Pier when one named Wyle, 6 years old, suddenly fell into the water. Attention was called to the accident when a young man, Wilson Beck, one of the harbour boatmen, went into the water to a considerable depth, and saw only a portion of the boy's coat. He reached down and got hold of it. By this means, he was got out, apparently dead and after great exertions and friction, he was restored to life.

We believe this is the third instance in which Beck has rescued young people from drowning.

13 October 1877 West Cumberland Times
Public Notices

Jane Wyle of Nelson Street, Maryport, returns her sincere thanks to Wilson Beck, Captain Conley, and others for their bravery in saving the life of her son, William Wyle, on Tuesday the 9th instant.

4 October 1879 Belfast Morning News
Personal Bravery

In a Maryport paper of last week, we find an account... of human greatness in humble life. Joseph Skelton, a foreman mason, was, with other workmen, employed repairing one of the bridges on the Maryport and Carlisle railway. While by means of a jib crane the men were raising a block of stone, about four hundred-weight, the jib lurched, and the stone fell right across the metals of the line. The up-train would be passing the spot in five minutes, and, calling on one of the stoutest of his men to aid him, Joseph Skelton set to work at once, and the huge obstruction was out of the way by some inches, when, round a curve, scarcely one hundred yards off, the train came rushing on, and passed as the foreman was swinging back the jib of the crane to keep it clear of the line. Swiftly sped the train, with its twenty carriages and their hundreds of passengers, but Joseph Skelton had been struck by the engine, and died in a few minutes. "Died," as our contemporary has it, "In the arms of duty, and in preventing a terribly extended disaster, and as nobly as any hero who fell in defending Rorke's Drift, or while fighting in the passes of Afghanistan…"

THE 1880s

15 December 1882 The Maryport Advertiser and Weekly News
Gallant Rescue by a Maryport Captain

For some time considerable anxiety has been felt in Maryport with respect to the safety of the barque *Abbey Holme* of this port. The vessel, which is owned by Messrs Hines Bros. of this town, sailed from Workington the 13th of October with a cargo of steel rails for Port Adelaide, South Australia. On the 8th of November a paragraph appeared in Lloyd's List, headed "Abbey Holme" and stating that the headboard of a ship with the name "Abbey Holme" on it, had washed ashore on Borth Beach, four miles to the south of Aberdovey; also that a quantity of small boards, forming part of a round house, had washed ashore at the same place, and that they appeared to have not been long in the water. In consequence of this paragraph, the under writers and a great many persons who had friends on board the *Abbey Holme* became very anxious, thinking probably that the vessel had collided with another vessel, or that some other accident had happened to her. The owners however were fully confident that the *Abbey Holme* was all right, and their confidence has been fully justified; for a Lloyd's telegram, dated Capetown 12 Dec. states that "the splendid iron, four-masted ship *Shakespeare* 1,814 tons register, owned in Liverpool, bound from Cardiff to Calcutta with a valuable cargo, had run aground on an inaccessible island - a reef of rocks in the South Atlantic Ocean - during a thick fog, and become a total wreck. The whole of the crew and passengers, 60 in number, were saved, and after spending several weeks on the island, were taken off by the *Abbey Holme* and landed at Simon's Bay on Tuesday.

As the Master, Captain JH Rich, the Mate, four crewmen and two apprentices on board the *Abbey Holme* belong to Maryport, the news of her safety will be hailed with pleasure.

10 November 1883 Wigton Advertiser
A Brave Deed Acknowledged

At a meeting of the Royal National Lifeboat Institution held the other day, the thanks of the Institution, inscribed on vellum, were accorded to Mr John Hutchings, the Chief Coastguard Officer at Maryport, for his bravery in saving lives from shipwreck, and notably for his going out in, and taken command of, the Maryport Lifeboat on September 26 whereby the crew of the steamer *Barrington* of Maryport, was saved.

The 'Barrington' had been driven onto the shore on the north side of the harbour entrance during a terrific south-westerly gale. She was a total wreck.

8 February 1884 Maryport Advertiser

The Bronze Medal of the Royal Humane Society was presented to Mr Antonio Treche of Maryport, by Mr HP Senhouse. Mr Treche was at the dockside in August of 1883 when a six year old boy called John Porthouse slipped and fell into the water. The presentation took place at the Athenaeum in Catherine Street; Mr Senhouse recounted the circumstances of Mr Treche's actions. Without hesitation he threw off his coat and boots, diving in to save the boy's life. Mr Treche had made Maryport his home, and had lived there for the last three years. Maryport, said Mr

Senhouse, was proud of him. Mr Treche was a ship-broker.

25 May 1887 West Cumberland Times
Bravery of a Maryport Clergyman

The Royal Humane Society has conferred its Silver Medal on the Rev JB Hewitson, East London missionary, for plunging into the Thames from a steamer, near Blackfriars Bridge, on the 13th ult. and attempting to save James Croydon, an old man of 80. Mr Hewitson is the son of Mrs Hewitson, Borroskill, near Maryport, and brother of Mr John Hewitson, Maryport.

26 August 1887 The Carlisle Patriot
A Gallant Rescue at Maryport

As the tide was going out on Saturday last, a girl named Thompson, aged eight years, fell into the Maryport Harbour and was being rapidly carried down towards the harbour bridge when a man named Joshua Hunter jumped into the water, with his clothes on, and rescued her.

3 April 1888 The Morning Post
Rescue from Drowning

At Maryport on Sunday evening, a clerk named John Hastings, was standing on the stones which lead from the Promenade to the sea, when he slipped and fell into the water. Two working men, John Davidson and Robert Reay, immediately dashed into the surf, and with great difficulty reached Hastings. All were for some time in peril, but ropes were thrown to them from the sea wall, and they were drawn ashore, much exhausted.

As Mr Hastings fell into the water, he hit the back of his head on stonework, which stunned him. The backwash of the water washed him away from the seawall, and he would have drowned soon. John Davidson went into the water to save him, but a great

wave separated them; Hastings was exhausted by now. Robert Reay then entered the water whilst a Mr Sharpe positioned himself on the stonework of the promenade. Standing up to his waist in sea-water, Sharpe held out his walking stick towards Reay. Holding Hastings's apparently lifeless body in one arm, Reay attempted to grasp the stick but could not grip it. Sharpe reversed the stick to offer the bent end and Reay seized it; this time Mr Sharpe could not hold it. The situation was now very dangerous, but someone brought a rope. Mr Sharpe called to Mr Reay to wind it round his arm; he did so and was dragged ashore, still holding Mr Hastings. At the same time Mr Davidson, who had been struggling in the water, managed to get himself to shore.

Mr Joseph Hodgson, a member of the St John's Ambulance organisation now made great efforts to bring Mr Hastings round, and after strenuous efforts, managed to get him breathing and conscious.

Mr Reay was awarded a testimonial on vellum by the Royal Humane Society whilst Mr Sharpe and Mr Hodgson received the same on parchment. In his speech of congratulations to the three men, Mr E Tyson stated that although the society had not chosen to present Mr Davidson with a parchment, he was sure that the people of Maryport recognised his bravery also, a statement which was met with "hear, hear!" by the audience.

30 May 1888 The West Cumberland Times
Rescue of a Drowning Man at Maryport

On Sunday morning, a labourer named Thompson, in attempting to reach the *Thorne Holme*, fell off the gangway and into the Senhouse Dock. A boat, in which were two boys, was in the immediate vicinity, and a young man named Henry Nutter, jumped into it and went to the assistance of Thompson, whose head he held above water until a line was thrown from the steamer. The rope was passed around Thompson's body, and he was safely hauled out of the water.

3 August 1888 Echo (London)
A Plucky Boy

At Grasslot, near Maryport yesterday, an exciting scene was witnessed. Several boys were bathing in a deep pond, when one of them, named Armstrong, began to sink. A comrade named Ellwood pluckily swam to his rescue, but Armstrong had disappeared beneath the surface before the other boy could reach him, and was drowned.

5 October 1888 Maryport Advertiser
Another Narrow Escape from Drowning

On Tuesday morning, the wife of James Ferguson, of Glasson, narrowly escaped being drowned. She was going on board the *River Clyde* lying in the Senhouse Dock, to obtain some clothes which she was expected to wash, when she fell into the water. She supported herself as well as she was able between the dock wall and the side of the vessel but in all probability she would have been drowned had not two men named Ben Brown and B Robinson gone to the rescue. She had been about three minutes in the water, and although it was a terribly cold morning, she was able to walk home.

27 November 1888 The Eastern Morning News
Exciting Scenes at Maryport
Rescue by a lifeboat

An exciting scene was witnessed off Maryport on Sunday afternoon. The Harbourmaster saw a vessel in distress in Solway Firth. The promenade and pier were soon crowded with people, amid cheers from whom the lifeboat was speedily launched and towed over the shore surf by the tug *Senhouse*. Whilst the lifeboat struggled in a tremendous sea, and against huge waves to reach the doomed vessel, the latter was constantly lost to view of those on shore, and a fear from time to time arose lest the rescuers risked their lives in vain. The latter, however, laboured manfully through the storm, and on nearing the vessel were greeted with a feeble cheer from fourteen exhausted members of the crew, lashed to the rocking masts. The stays of the latter were all gone and the men's position

17

became momentarily more perilous. The ship was covered above-decks with sand and water, and the lifeboat had difficulty reaching her owing to the floating wreckage. At length all the men were safely got on board, two having been only narrowly saved. They were lashed together, and at an inaccessible part of the rigging. A life-line was thrown them, and as their only chance, they leapt into the sea. After a desperate struggle with the waves, they were rescued breathless and exhausted. The lifeboat then returned and reached the shore, amid the deafening cheers of the spectators. The rescued crew were terribly exhausted. They had been lashed to the masts with the sea beating over them for eight hours. They were cared for by the local agent of the Shipwrecked Mariners' Society. The wrecked vessel was the barque *Estrella de Chili.* She left Whitehaven for the River Plate with a cargo of steel rails on Friday and was driven back by adverse winds on Saturday midnight into the Solway, where she became fixed on the Robin Rigg sandbank. Soon after striking here, the mate was washed overboard and drowned.

THE 1890s

31 January 1891 Maryport Advertiser

It was on Saturday 31 January, when the Cumbrian coast was hit by a hurricane between two and three in the morning. Luckily, the tide was going out or disaster would have ensued as mountainous waves drove in fury up the beaches, roaring off rocks and attacking harbours with raging force. Maryport felt the full impact of the wind as chimney pots fell, slates dislodged, and near the coast, the pounding of the waves caused some houses to shake so that their inhabitants left their beds in a state of alarm. The roof of the schoolroom in Station Street, which was in the

process of being constructed, fell and was reduced to splinters. Out at sea, at the mercy of titanic nature, was a small trawler out of Whitehaven, called The Wave. She made way as best as she could, for the safety of Maryport Harbour, but as she neared her destination, the wind blew most of the sails away and shredded what was left.

Onshore, the trawler was seen to be in difficulties and the maroons were sent up to summon the lifeboat crew. As the sharp cracks of the rockets sounded across the town, the lifeboatmen hurried down to take their posts, and hundreds of people went down to see what was happening. Unable to make the mouth of the harbour, The Wave was driven onto the north shore the where she grounded. The water was not more than four or five feet deep, but such was the violence of the sea that no man could stand in it.

A huge crowd gathered onshore and watched in horror as the vessel pounded up and down on the ground, threatening to be broken to pieces at any moment. At this point a group of local men, roped together, waded into water up to their necks, and carried a rope halfway to the wreck. In the howling of the wind they could not make themselves heard but gesticulated to the men on the trawler to jump in and move towards the rope. They did not do so, it being too far for them. Charles Smith, a Sergeant in the Artillery Reserve, seeing this, walked further towards the wreck with the rope, so that the water came over his head; he had to be assisted back to shore.

*Samuel Hardingham now fought his way through
the waves and managed to board the trawler where he
urged the crew to save their lives and jump for the
rope. Just then the Maryport Lifeboat came round
from the harbour, and the crew thought that a better
option. Hardingham left them and, to show how it was
possible, came ashore using the rope.*

*The lifeboat was rowed by strong men, but the sea
was merciless. John Benn was the Coxswain, and his
crew were Charles McCartney, William Kirkbride
(Senior), W Kirkbride (Junior), Joseph Kirkbride,
Charles McGerry, John Johnstone, Joseph
Lewthwaite, Robert Mantle, John Messenger, Samuel
McGran, Henry Waugh and J Robinson. The*

lifeboatmen fought hard and cast an anchor to windward of the wreck, but the force of the waves drifted her to leeward. The anchor had dragged and now the lifeboat itself was at risk; she sent up red rockets, indicating distress. The lifeboat was now in danger of being dashed ashore at Bank End, so most of the watching crowd, seeing their friends and relations' predicament, rushed over there.

Observing this, the men of The Wave now tried to lower their own boat, in which they succeeded. No sooner had they all got in than it filled with water and sank. The trawlermen scrambled back onto the wreck as best they could.

As the exhausted men managed to get back onto the wreck, Captain Nelson, the Harbourmaster, Captain Winterton of the Arbatus, John Little, Michael Hawkins and Thomas Reay appeared from the harbour in a light skiff. In view of the crowd, they took the men on board and headed straight for shore where willing hands hauled the skiff in, and brought everyone safely to firm ground.

In the meantime, the lifeboat had managed to cut the rope to the anchor which was dragging them, and despite breaking an oar, succeeded in turning the head of the boat away from shore. Heading out into deep water, they put up their sail and set course for Silloth, Maryport being impossible. The boat repeatedly filled in the rough seas and had to be baled out constantly. Eventually they reached Silloth, where they were received with all possible kindness.

Coxswain 'Lion-hearted' Benn

14 February 1891
The Recent Wreck at Maryport

The National Lifeboat Institution have forwarded £6 to be divided amongst the men who took part in the rescuing of the crew of the *"Wave"* of Whitehaven, at Maryport during the last storm. Captain Nelson. Captain Winterton, Mr J Ferguson, Mr M Hawkins, and Mr J Little, who manned the skiff get 10s each. Mr SJ Hardingham (of the naval reserve), Mr Charles Smith (of the Artillery Volunteers), Mr J Dixon, Mr B Davis and Mr H Tremble, who attempted a rescue by means of a rope, get 10s each; and Mr H Reay, Mr A McEwen, Mr D Harbourne and Mr Armstrong, who assisted in the rescue, get 5s each. There has also been sent £1 15s to divide amongst the crew of the small vessel that towed the lifeboat from Silloth to Maryport. The matter was brought before the Committee of the Institution in London by the report of Captain Penrice, the secretary at Maryport, and they very properly saw fit to make the above awards.

December 1892

In 1892, an iron Barque, 'Aikshaw,' owned by Captain Edward Tyson, of Maryport, and commanded by Captain Cobb, and carrying coal, was caught in a gale and driven onto sunken rocks on the coast of Chile. The ship heeled over on her side, strong seas breaking over her so that it was only a matter of time until all would be swept away. This happened to five men, all of whom drowned. Mr Daniel Turney, the Second Mate, of Maryport, saw that the mainmast was over some rocks on the land. He crawled along the mast and dropped onto the rocks. Amidst the howling gale and waves, he then encouraged and assisted members of the crew onto the land, saving most of the crew.

Turney and the rescued crew took ship for home on the steamship 'John Elder.' Twenty-four hours after leaving Valparaiso the ship ran upon some rocks and was completely wrecked. The captain and crew of the 'Aikshaw' assisted the officers of the 'John Elder' in saving the lives of the passengers. For this action, Turney was also awarded the testimonial parchment of the Royal Humane Society for saving life at sea.

Daniel Turney later joined an Australian shipping line as a captain.

The brass bell of the 'Aikshaw' was recovered in 1930.

14 May 1893 Maryport Advertiser
Gallantry of a Maryport Man
Presentation of the Board of Trade's Silver Medal

On Monday night a public meeting was held at the town and harbour office, Maryport, in connection with the presentation of the Board of Trade's Silver Medal to Mr DS Turney, late Second Mate of the barque *Aikshaw* for gallantry in saving life when the ship was wrecked in sight of the harbour of Antofagasta, South America in December last...

17 June 1893 The West Cumberland Times

On Tuesday, a person named Henry Hartley fell into the Senhouse Dock basin. A man named Woodhouse jumped in and rescued him.

1 December 1893 The Carlisle Journal
Rescue of a Crew by a Maryport Steamer

Messrs. Hine's steamer the *Nether Holme* arrived in London on Saturday, having on board the crew of the Norwegian barque, the *Roskna,* which she had picked up some distance east of the Banks of Newfoundland. The *Roskna*, when sighted, was in a waterlogged condition, and would doubtless have foundered had it not been for the fact that she was timber-laden. A boat was lowered from the *Nether Holme* and the dozen men forming the Norwegian's crew taken off, an operation which the storm then raging made one of considerable danger. When off the Scilly Isles, the *Nether Holme* passed the hull of a ship, floating bottom up.

5 August 1893 The West Cumberland Times
A Plucky Rescue by a Lady

A Larne newspaper says: Last week while a number of young ladies were bathing at the Bank Heads, one of them took cramp when a good distance from the shore, and, but for the timely assistance rendered by Miss McCully (daughter of Captain McCully, Clonlee) a fatal accident might have occurred. Miss McCully deserves to be warmly congratulated on her plucky rescue of the lady, who, we understand, is a summer visitor to our town. Miss

McCully's mother is a native of Maryport, where the young lady has visited on several occasions, and where she is well known.

26 January 1895 The West Cumberland Times
Gallant Rescue at Maryport

On Sunday afternoon last, as a number of young men were having a walk round the docks at Maryport, one of them spied the top of a man's hat above the water in the Senhouse Dock. Calling the attention of his mates, they imagined that a head might be inside so they determined to fish out the 'tile' at whatever risk. Going to the high end of the dock they procured a boat and set out on their errand of mercy. Some of the rescuers were well-known members of the Maryport Rugby Club but they soon showed that they could not scull so well as they can scrimmage. A heavy breeze was blowing in from the east, and, after attempting to drive the boat in the teeth of it for ten minutes without seeming to move, the others on the quay took them in tow and they at last reached the desired goal. Arrived in position, a trio of willing hands was stretched out from the boat and the parcel was easily lifted out of the water, when the astonished watchers were rewarded by seeing - not a hat with a head in it, but only a hat. Visions of promotion and fame at once melted from their view, and they each looked as if they would have liked to have kicked the head which should have been in the hat, and possibly even felt willing to kick themselves. However, the spectators took the will for the deed and cheered the rescuers to the echo.

13 February 1895 West Cumberland Times
A Brave Cumberland Lad
A Gritty Young Upholsterer

The following is taken from the *"San Francisco Examiner"* and may be interesting to our readers, referring as it does, to a young Cumbrian. "Albert Winslow, an apprentice at the upholstering firm of Charles M Plum & Co. had his arm badly broken and lacerated by a hair-picking machine yesterday afternoon.

He was working over the machine, which carried a number of wondrous looking teeth, when he slipped on some oil on the floor, and, in an effort to save himself from falling, foolishly clutched at the machine. The teeth seized hold of the sleeve of his shirt, drew his left arm in, and, and mangled it horribly. The arm clogged in the machine, however, for the power used is weak. A fellow workman saw poor Winslow's plight, and summoned assistance. It was found impossible to liberate the lad without taking the machine to pieces. To do this, it was necessary to saw through a 4x4 beam, and a rod of iron, with almost no tools at hand. Winslow, though in intense agony, encouraged the workers, directing their movements, and telling them not to hurry. The boy is only 17 years of age. His heroism was greatly admired. It took twenty-five minutes to get him free from the teeth, and he was then conveyed to the City Receiving Hospital, where it was found the arm had suffered a compound comminuted fracture, and severe laceration. The bones were set, and Winslow was put to bed in the hospital."

We are indebted to a Wigtonian, now resident in Frisco for the following additional particulars:- The young man's real name is Hunter. He is the son of Mrs Mary Jane Winslow, a daughter of the late Mr Joseph Ward, painter, well known in Wigton and Maryport. After the death of her husband, Mr William Hunter, of Maryport, she went to San Francisco to join her brother Tom there, and some time after married Mr Winslow of the United States Revenue Service, and formerly of the US Navy. He was recently granted a pension by that government.

At the receiving station the surgeons concluded that amputation was necessary. Mrs Winslow, who had considerable experience in Cumberland and in the States as a hospital and private nurse, deemed it prudent to call in an independent physician, and Dr Gilbert, an English practitioner, was summoned. He was of the opinion that the limb might be preserved, and the youth was accordingly removed to a private hospital. When the British mail left on the 24th, Winslow's condition was more hopeful than at any other period since his accident.

Unfortunately there is no extant evidence as to what happened to Albert's arm, and the newspaper did not do a follow up article.

15 August 1895 Liverpool Shipping Telegraph and Daily Commercial Advertiser
Bravery at sea

At the Mercantile Marine Office, Penarth, Cardiff, on Tuesday morning, two presentations took place for bravery in the open sea. William Farrell, Master of the barque *Gladstone,* Maryport, was presented with a handsome gold watch and chain for gallantry under the following circumstances:- The *Gladstone* sighted the *Felix Mendelsohn* about 300 miles west of the Azores, in distress; there was a tremendously heavy sea on, but despite this, all on board the *Felix Mendelsohn,* who were in desperate condition, were rescued, and, afterwards, landed at Queenborough. Mr M Kruger, on behalf of the German government, made eulogistic reference to the bravery of Captain Farrell.

The 'Felix Mendelsohn' had left Pensicola, Florida in November 1892. On 21 December, she was hit by a hurricane which dismasted her, and heaved her over so much that though she righted, she was water-logged. Everything loose had been swept away, including the ship's boats. All fresh water, and provisions were spoiled. A seaman was washed

30

overboard, and the carpenter died. They drifted for six days, surviving on some rice the men had found, and rainwater. By this time the sea was washing over the wreck, and she was beginning to break up. On 27 December a barque passed by them, and did not stop.

Some hours later the despairing crew saw another barque and used their last match to light their last blue flare. If it had not been answered then all hope would have been lost. As they watched, the barque took in sail and rounded to. It was the 'Gladstone' a Maryport ship, crewed mostly by Cumbrians. The night was setting in and the sea very angry, so the Germans thought that no rescue could be made until morning. They watched amazed as the Maryport men launched a boat and came towards them. It was commanded by the Mate, Mr Brydges, and crewed by volunteers. They did the journey between the two ships twice and brought all twelve men on the 'Felix Mendelsohn' safely aboard the 'Gladstone'.

Each man in the ship's boat received £3 reward for their part in the rescue and Mr Brydges also received a gold watch and chain.

23 November 1895 West Cumberland Times
Recognition of Bravery at Maryport
A Gallant Rescue

Two Maryport fishermen named Charles Smith and James Burns have been the recipients of £1 each, presented by the Royal National Lifeboat Institution, through the local secretary, Mr Q Moore, as a reward for their gallantry in rescuing a fellow fisherman, named William Tyndall, from drowning on the 15th ult. On the morning of that date Tyndall left Maryport alone to fish in his small boat. Upon returning in the afternoon it was very wild, and in making the harbour at almost dead low water, the strong wind and the heavy freshet which was running out, swamped the boat. Tyndall was observed clinging to the mast of the boat by Smith and Burns who went to his rescue. They succeeded in transferring him safely to their boat, but in their attempt to return, they were driven out to sea three times and were almost swamped. Each time they were compelled to anchor and bale the water out of their craft. Finally, however, they succeeded into getting into port. The exciting incident was brought under the notice of Mr Q Moore, who forwarded the particulars to the Royal National Lifeboat Institution, and at their Board meeting it was unanimously decided to forward a cheque for £2 to be divided between the men.

11 April 1896 The West Cumberland Times
Honour to a Maryport sailor

Word has been received that a silver medal, the gift of the Norwegian government, has arrived at London, to be presented to Mr Thomas Raby, a native of Maryport, who is on board an East Indian trader, the

SS Larnaca, for gallant services rendered in rescuing life at sea.

16 July 1896 Cumberland Pacquet and Ware's Whitehaven Advertiser
Bravery to be Rewarded at Maryport

A public meeting will be held in the Town Hall, Maryport, on Monday 20th inst. at seven pm. when Mr Senhouse will present to Mr Joseph Higgins a testimonial inscribed on vellum, awarded by the Royal Humane Society, for saving life on 11 May last.

Mr Higgins jumped into 27 feet of water in the Senhouse dock to save Horace Freestone, a boy who had fallen in.

6 February 1897
A Heroic Maryport Engineer

The "Belgian News and Times" contains a report of the presentation of two civic crosses of the first and second classes respectively, to Captain Evans, Master, and Mr Rich, Chief Engineer of the *SS Rich* at the office of the British Consulate at Antwerp. The decorations were awarded by the Belgian government in recognition of the services of the two officers on the occasion of the rescue of the crew of the Belgian *SS Princess Clementine,* in the month of June 1896. The Consul-General, in making the presentation, said: "The very pleasing duty has devolved on me today of delivering to two fellow countrymen the insignia and diplomas of the Belgian Civic Cross. The distinction conferred by these decorations is, as you are doubtless aware, a very considerable one. They are, in fact, only awarded in recognition of acts of Conspicuous Gallantry and of marked devotion to duty... Mr Rich, whose residence is in Christian Street, is well known in Maryport, being a son of Capt. Rich of the barque *Briar Holme.* "

The 'Princess Clementine' was in collision off Bordeaux, at the mouth of the Gironde, and suffered a large hole in her stern. She sank almost immediately after colliding with the Swedish barque 'Axel Wastfelt', and her crew took to her boats, but some fell into the water. A gale was blowing, with a heavy sea. The steamer 'Rex' was nearby, and made strenuous efforts to save the people struggling to live. Mr GJ Jenkins, First Mate of the 'Rex' had himself lowered over the side with a rope round his waist so that he could physically drag men from the waves; a process during which he was frequently submerged. Mr David Jones, the Second Mate took a boat out onto the rough seas and saved more; they rescued fifteen in all, though sadly the captain of the 'Princess Clementine' was drowned. Captain Evans, Mr Jenkins, and Mr Jones all received the Silver Medal of the Liverpool Shipwreck and Humane Society.

18 September 1897 Maryport Advertiser
Narrow Escape of a Child at Maryport
A Gallant Rescue from Drowning

At noon on Saturday, a boy two-and-a-half years old, son of Mr Robert Plaskett, miller, Furnace Mill, Maryport, had a narrow escape from drowning. The River Ellen flows close past Furnace Mill, and, as there is no protection at the end of the sawmill, the place is very dangerous for children, especially when the tide is in.

The little boy had been playing with a number of neighbouring children and an elderly woman named

35

Mrs Wilson was sitting on a log of timber within a few yards of the water side, but no-one heard or saw him fall into the water. At this time, Charles Minshaw Jnr. was working at a cart on the timber hill, adjoining the sawmill, and, inferring from the noise and confusion that someone had fallen into the water, he hastened round the sawmill, divesting himself as he ran of his waistcoat and hat. When he reached the river side, the child, after going under the water twice, was swirling in the stream some twenty feet from the side. Plunging into the water Minshaw, in a few seconds, brought the child, in a complete state of collapse, safely ashore and handed it over to its mother.

The West Cumberland Times of 24 November 1897 reported that Charles Minshaw was awarded a parchment in vellum from the Royal Humane Society. Mr Minshaw received his scroll at the town hall where there was much applause and many congratulations for his bravery.

31 December 1897 Carlisle Journal
Vessel in Distress in the Solway
Bravery of Maryport Seamen

The schooner *Mary Ellen,* bound for Maryport, to load coals for Belfast, took refuge at Silloth on Sunday. It appears that shortly after noon on Sunday, while a strong wind was blowing from the south-west, and a tremendous sea running, the schooner attempted to enter the harbour at Maryport, but was driven onto the north side of the concrete pier, where the anchors were dropped. The steam-tug *Senhouse* went to the assistance of the schooner and got her in tow, but the tow-rope broke, and the vessel was in great danger of being driven ashore, as one anchor had been slipped when the tug took her in charge. In this predicament, the captain called for a pilot to run the schooner to Silloth, and William Kirkbride, a veteran close on 80 years of age, who is always to the fore in an emergency, and who has saved a long list of men from wrecked vessels, along with his son William, and two other fishermen named Ferguson and Reay, went out

37

in an open boat, at fearful peril and succeeded in putting William Kirkbride Jun. on board.

By this time the vessel had drifted towards the tan-yard and would soon have been ashore, but Kirkbride lost no time in ordering the remaining anchor to be slipped, and he headed the vessel off shore, and made for Silloth, reaching that port safely an hour or so later.

11 February 1899 West Cumberland Times

It is somewhere verging on fifty years since the vessel *John Ritson* left Maryport with a party of emigrants for California. Probably the incident might have gradually sunk out of ken, even in the minds of relatives of those who ventured out to the land of gold, if it had not been owing to a letter of enquiry from over the water respecting the full particulars of the ship *John Ritson,* which was a Maryport vessel, and her complement of passengers and crew. It appears that a movement is on foot among the survivors to celebrate the Jubilee of their setting foot in California. The letter was addressed to the Post Office, and eventually came into the hands of Mr John Curwen, who, with the aid of a few relatives of those who went out, has forwarded the necessary particulars. Half a century is a long period to look back, and it would be interesting to know how many of the daring voyagers … have survived. …

It is a matter of regret that the celebration of the Jubilee could not pass over without some reference to the sad incident which occurred immediately after landing. Captain George Kennedy was in command of the vessel, and, after arrival out there, he was going ashore in a small boat accompanied by the apprentices, when the boat capsized. Captain Kennedy was an expert swimmer, and he struggled to right the boat, which he eventually succeeded in doing. His next effort was to save the apprentices, and he was successful, but unfortunately he was unable to save himself. His heroic and self-sacrificing efforts had exhausted him, and after he had put the last apprentice into the boat, he was unable to battle with the waves, one of which carried him away and he was never heard of again. He was the only person drowned; but more would have been lost of it had not been for his noble exertions. It is trusted that the survivors, in their merriment will not overlook this deed of heroism, but will pay a due meed of praise to him who sacrificed his life to save others.

THE 1900s

8 June 1901 Maryport Advertiser
Reward for Gallantry at Maryport

On Saturday morning, Mr J Samuel, Superintendent of Mercantile Marine, presented Mr John Johnston, 20, Well Lane, Maryport, with a silver medal (second class) and a diploma from the Norwegian government as a reward for gallantry. Mr Samuel delivered a few appropriate words, and Mr Johnston replied. Mr Johnston was boatswain on board the *SS Verano,* and the following are the circumstances under which the officers and crew receive tokens of appreciation from the Norwegian government.

The ship *Verano* left Baltimore for Rotterdam on January 26th 1899 and encountered very bad weather during the whole passage. On the 8th February the weather moderated a little, but there was a very high sea. At three o'clock pm, the crew sighted a barque in distress, which proved to be the *Brilliant,* of Christiansund, on passage to Hamburg, with timber. The vessel had no distress signals flying, and it was concluded - as afterwards proved to be the case - that the crew, who were seen huddled together on the cabin top, with the sea going right over them, were too exhausted to make any signals. The *Verano* rounded so as to close with the wreck, poured oil on the sea, and launched the starboard lifeboat - the port one had been lost previously - in charge of the chief officer and five men, who, after a hard struggle, got a line attached to the Norwegian vessel, the crew of which, one by one, to the number of 13, jumped overboard with a line around their waists, and were got into the lifeboat. They were got into the *Verano* by the same means, as they could not do much for themselves, and the sea was high, and the lifeboat could not come alongside without great danger to the occupants- indeed, while it was being hoisted in afterwards, it was badly stove. The crew of the *Brilliant* had not had anything to eat for five days except wet biscuits, and they had nothing to drink. It was with difficulty they could be prevented from drinking too much afterwards, and all their hands and feet were terribly swollen, causing them great agony as soon as they became warm in bed. Scarcely had they been taken on board the *Verano* when it began to blow severely, but towards daylight the weather moderated.

29 June 1901 Maryport Advertiser
An Ambulance Man's Bravery

Bert Warren, a member of the Dalton St John's Ambulance Association, and son of Mr WT Warren, insurance agent, formerly of Maryport and Aspatria, saved a man from drowning. The man fell into the dock at Barrow from a height of 20 or 30 feet into water 20 feet deep. Warren jumped in, and landed the drowning man on some timber. He struggled hard and both were again precipitated into the dock. Warren however, succeeded in holding his man's head above the water until assistance arrived, and both were hauled out. The rescued man was unconscious, but before Warren left work he had the satisfaction of seeing him regain sensibility. Warren was presented with 10s as a mark of appreciation of one of the foremen of the yard. Recently, at a commanding officer's parade, Captain Pooley detailed the circumstances of Pvt. Warren's brave deed, and called for three cheers for Warren. The cheers were heartily given, and subsequently Captain Pooley commended Warren in suitable terms.

20 July 1901 Manchester Courier
Sad Sequel (sic) to a Gallant Rescue

A married woman, named Ann Lowes, living at Fothergill, near Maryport, died on Tuesday as the result of injuries received in an extraordinary accident. On Monday, Lowes, while picking coal at Risehow, from a heap of refuse coal, which is on fire, broke through the crust into the burning portion, which is below, and after struggling some time, rolled down the burning bank into the sea, the tide being very full at the time. A young man named Joseph McLauchlin courageously rushed down the bank at great peril from the breaking through of the surface, and, plunging into the sea, he rescued the unfortunate woman, who was found to be severely burned. McLauchlin's plucky conduct is the subject of much admiration.

27 August 1901 West Cumberland Times

It was reported that Captain Espie Dods, of the Queensland Army Medical Corps did some especially brave work. It was reported that Corporal Conley had been hit by Boer rifle fire in the South African war, so Captain Dods rode out through severe gunfire, to his assistance, but found that he had died. He then rode to Private Reece, but found he was also dead. Then he heard that Private Strong had been wounded, so once again he rode out, regardless of rifle fire, and tended to the wounded man on the battlefield. There was no hurry to him, just the professional coolness that one would expect from a doctor in one of the ordinary hospitals in his own country. Ten years before this, and before emigrating to Australia, Captain Dods had been assistant to Doctor Crerar GP in Maryport.

12 July 1902 The Maryport Advertiser
Plucky Rescue at Maryport

On Saturday a lad named James Cunningham, six years of age, fell into Maryport Harbour at full tide. On the alarm being raised, a young horse dealer named Sloan, who lives at Quay Side, was quickly on

the scene, and, plunging in, speedily rescued the child
who was none the worse for his dip.

2 August 1902 The Maryport Advertiser
Plucky Rescue at Maryport

On Friday afternoon, a child named Courtney went
into the water close to Timber Hill Maryport, and, as
the tide was ebbing, soon got into difficulties. Thomas
Miller, Richmond Yard, quickly divested himself of
his coat and clogs, and swam out to the child, which
by that time had been carried 40 or 50 yards away. He
succeeded in getting hold of the child and bringing it
to shore where he handed it over to John Courtney, the

father. Dr Proud was afterwards called in, and the child was brought around. Miller performed a plucky rescue and is worthy of commendation.

27 October 1902 Lancashire Evening Post
The Recent Wreck at Maryport
Reward for Gallantry

The Board of Trade have awarded their Bronze Medal for gallantry in saving life at sea to John Hampson, a member of the Royal Naval Reserve stationed at Maryport, for his services on the occasion of the wreck of the *Wild Rose*, of Liverpool, at Maryport on September 3rd last, in obtaining communication with the vessel, carrying the master's wife ashore on his back, through the surf, and assisting the crew to land.

29 July 1903 West Cumberland Times
Plucky Rescue at Maryport

Shortly after noon yesterday (Tuesday) a little girl named Thompson, who resides at Furnace Mill, fell into the River Ellen, which passes that place. The tide was in and the water was running swiftly. Luckily, Mr William Minshaw observed the accident, and pluckily jumped into the water and brought the child to the bank, apparently little the worse for her immersion. Mr Minshaw is to be complimented for the

45

promptness with which he jumped into the river,

which is dangerous at this place.

12 October 1904 West Cumberland Times
Maryport Man's Gallantry Abroad
Boy Pluckily Rescued from Drowning

An act of gallantry recently by a Maryport man -
Mr David Kennedy, son of Mr A Kennedy, Senhouse
Street, Maryport, and Second Steward of the *SS
Bonavista,* is recorded by the Newfoundland and other
papers. The boat was within five minutes of the time
for leaving the harbour of St John's Newfoundland,

when a little boy named McCoubrey, who with his mother was seeing a friend off by the SS *Bonavista,* fell over the gangway between the wharf and the steamer. The boat being scarcely two feet from the pier, the boy's position was a very perilous one, but a large number of people, with willing hands, kept the steamer from off the pier. The Steward Kennedy, seeing the boy's danger, jumped from the bridge down between the boat and the shore - a distance of some twelve feet - and, though the spectators feared both must surely be crushed to death, he "dextrously managed to squeeze in between the piers and land the boy unhurt".

In recognition of this brave act, performed at risk of his own life, Mr Kennedy, on arriving at Montreal, was presented with the Royal Humane Society's Medal for Distinguished Bravery, the passengers having signed a petition to obtain it for him. Mr and Mrs McCoubrey (the boy's parents) also evinced their deep gratitude to Mr Kennedy for his plucky saving of their boy's life, by sending him a letter of thanks, a handsomely mounted photograph of their boy, and another handsome gift, which will doubtless be henceforward numbered among Mr Kennedy's most treasured possessions.

One paper commenting on the occurrence says: "Kennedy has done many plucky acts of this nature, and on the pier today his bravery was highly commended." Another observes: "Steward Kennedy... will be presented with an RMS Medal on returning to Montreal, but as in the effort (of rescuing the boy) his gold watch was flung out of his pocket and lost, some of those interested should head a movement to present him with another".

Mr Kennedy, who resides at Halifax, Nova Scotia, has been abroad for eight years now. He is locally well known.

10 November 1906 West Cumberland Times
Fire at Maryport

About 8.15 on Tuesday night, a fire broke out in the back attic of the house above Mr Collin's sweet shop, at the bottom of Senhouse Street, Maryport, occupied by Mr and Mrs Preston. The youngest of the family, a little boy of five, was asleep in the room in bed at the time. He seems to have wakened up just in time, and his cries were heard by his sister Olive Cassandra (Cassie), aged 11, who, thinking he was disturbing them unnecessarily, ran upstairs shouting what she would do with him when she got to him. But when she reached the room, she found it full of smoke and flame. Nothing daunted, the little girl bravely rushed through it, and, seizing her brother, carried him on the landing and then downstairs. The boy escaped unhurt, but his sister had her nose burned and face scorched. But for the gallant action of his sister, the little boy would probably have been suffocated. There were only three children in the house at the time, the two mentioned, and Martha, an elder sister, aged 13, the father, who is a marine engineer, being away at sea, and the mother being out. In the meantime Miss Bell, manageress of Mr Collin's shop below, raised the alarm and informed Mr George Armstrong, pork butcher, who lives next door. The latter rushed into the house, and, with the assistance of a young man who worked very hard, Mr WE Mandle, the owner of the property, and others, the fire was got under. *(control)* Mr Armstrong fortunately had a large tub of water standing in his yard, and thus there was more water immediately available than would otherwise have been the case. The Fire Brigade arrived very speedily on the scene with the hose reel, but the latter was never called into requisition.

The bedding and some clothes belonging to Mr Preston that were in a box in the room, were burned, damage being done to the extent of £10 or £15. The gas pipe was burned through, and other damage done to the room.

23 November 1906 The Yorkshire Post
A Wreck Off Maryport
Lifeboat Rescue of Twenty-One Men

On 21 November 1906 the *SS Greyfield* of London entered the Solway Firth. She was commanded by Captain Tyson and owned by Messrs Evan Jones and Co. of Cardiff. Her cargo was 3000 tons of iron ore from Poti in Georgia. Unfortunately the weather was appalling and the *Greyfield* was unable to pick up a pilot. Captain Tyson decided that it would be best to drop anchor and ride out the storm. As darkness came, the force of the wind grew so high that the ship began to drag her anchor and eventually drifted onto Robin Rigg, a sandbank notorious for wrecking ships.

Now the *Greyfield* sent up distress rockets which were seen from Maryport; the lifeboat crew was summoned by the maroons at once, and the boat set off at 9.30 pm. The tide was dead low and the boat had to be manhandled over sand until she could reach sufficient water to launch. It was not until after 11 pm that there was enough water for the lifeboat to leave the harbour, and the crew rowed her out into a howling south-westerly gale and into pitch blackness. The night was so wild that the lifeboatmen could not locate the wreck for some time, but eventually some more rockets allowed them to find the *Greyfield*. The stricken ship was heeled over on the sandbank with heavy seas sweeping over her. Despite this the lifeboatmen tried repeatedly to approach the wreck, but were in danger of having their boat dashed to pieces against the side of the ship.

There was no other choice but to beat about the wreck until the tide ebbed enough to allow a safe approach. This was not for over an hour but eventually the lifeboat was able to run into the lee of the ship; there they held until every man was able to leap to safety. There followed a long hard row back to Maryport; no-one had died and the rescuers landed the stricken crew safely at 6.30 am. It had been a hard night.

The shipwrecked men were suffering from cold, exposure and lack of food. The men were accommodated at the Coffee Tavern and the officers at the *Golden Lion.*

On 1 June 1907 a man walking on the beach near Flimby picked up a bottle which had a message in it. It read as follow, "SS Greyfield. No hope. We are sinking on Robin Rigg. If this should come into the hands of any well-disposed person, please tell my brother, whose name is John Graham of Seaforth in

Devonshire, that I, William Graham, Third Mate, leave all my property to him. William Graham No hope."

This is a measure of how desperate the situation was, yet Maryport Lifeboat saved them all.

1 January 1908 The Staffordshire Sentinel
Invalid in a Burning House
Rescue by Ladder at Maryport

A fire occurred on Tuesday at a house in John Street, Maryport, occupied by Mrs Abbot, an aging widow, who is an invalid. Her son and daughter were attending a funeral. Mrs Abbot appeared at a window in her bed attic and two men named Storey and Irving obtained a ladder, and climbing up, succeeded in getting her out. Police Inspector Towey backed a passing cart onto the footway and this served as a platform on which several men stood and took Mrs Abbot from the hands of her rescuers. She was but little the worse for the occurrence.

The redoubtable Mr Wilson Beck has appeared in this book before; he certainly was a very brave man. He does appear however, several times in the newspapers because he appeared in front of the magistrates through being drunk. His habit seems to have cost him his job as a harbour boatman, whereupon he took to the sea, and survived a

*shipwreck; he could evidently swim like a fish. In
1908 he appeared in front of the magistrates again.*

12 December 1908 Lancashire Evening Post
Maryport Hero in the Dock

At Maryport yesterday, Wilson Beck (55) Mariner,
Maryport, was charged on remand with doing
grievous bodily harm to his son, Chambers Beck, by
throwing a lighted lamp at him on the 24th ult. The
charge was reduced to one of common assault by the
police, and the prisoner pleaded guilty.

Mr Crerar, for the defence, said both men were
intoxicated. Prisoner, in the course of his life, had
saved between 30 and 40 people from drowning in the
Maryport Docks, and deserved well of his townsmen.
It would be an act of mercy to let him go forth.

The magistrates dismissed the case on payment of
costs (7s).

19 July 1909 The Sheffield Daily Independent
Miners Overcome

The "Daily News" Maryport correspondent says
that a thrilling accident, followed by an extraordinary
rescue, has occurred in the Moorhouse Guards
Colliery, West Cumberland.

Three men- John Wood, of Flimby and Jas. Francis
and his son, of Seaton, were engaged in clearing out
an old airshaft, and Wood descended in a small kibble

or tub. As he failed to respond to the signals of those above, it was concluded that he must have been rendered unconscious by gas.

Young Francis pluckily volunteered to go down to his assistance, making a perilous descent by the rope. He in turn must have collapsed, for there was no sign to those above that he had been able to help Wood.

The father of the youth, after giving the alarm to others on the surface, prepared to go down the rope himself. He dropped out of sight, and it soon became evident that he had shared the fate of the two already below.

No-one else dared venture down. At last, after a lapse of twenty minutes, in despair of doing anything better, it was decided to haul up the kibble. Its weight taxed the strength of the rescuers, and when at last it emerged from the shaft, the three men came with it, each hanging over the side unconscious, with one foot locked in the tub.

THE 1910s

24 April 1910 Weekly Dispatch (London)
Brother's Heroic Rescue

A fire broke out in a bedroom of Mr JH Timoney, the well-known Cumberland Northern Union football player, and captain of the Maryport club, and destroyed all the club's jerseys and clothes, together with Timoney's county cap. Mr and Mrs Timoney were away at her father's death bed, and three children who were asleep in the house had a narrow escape. John, aged thirteen, heroically rescued his brother Tom by carrying him downstairs. Sarah, aged eight, was rescued by a neighbour named Robert Monan. Mrs Timoney's father died while the fire was in progress.

5 October 1910 West Cumberland Times

On Monday night at a concert held in the Seamans' Institute, Maryport, George Wilson, a Maryport young man, was presented with the parchment of the Royal Humane Society, for having rescued a boy named John Gilmour from drowning in Maryport Harbour on April 14th last.

Mr GJP Senhouse, who presided at the concert, made the presentation. He said they would all know the details of the brave act for which Mr Wilson was to receive the certificate. They must understand that

Mr Wilson was not a sailor, but what the sailor would call a landlubber. All in Maryport would be very proud of him (applause).

The certificate was handed over and Mr Wilson modestly returned thanks.

13 September 1912 Millom Gazette
Maryport Child Drowned

Leslie Slater, the two year old son of John William Slater, a well-known Cumberland Association footballer, fell into Maryport Harbour on Tuesday, and was drowned.

William French, a Northern Union player, made a gallant attempt at rescue. He plunged into a strong ebb tide and brought the child to the quay, but all efforts to restore animation failed.

The jury, in returning a verdict of "Accidentally drowned" commended French's bravery.

1 January 1913 West Cumberland Times
Maryport Boy's Freak

A boyish prank on the part of a Maryport youngster named Smith, six years of age, living in Furnace Lane, nearly ended in his being drowned on Saturday afternoon. The boy was with some companions playing on the banks of the River Ellen in the field along the Mealpot Road. Encouraged, it is said, by some of those who were with him, he took off his

clothes and went into the river to bathe. Normally the water at this place is shallow, but at the time of the incident, half past two, the tide was full and the river was considerably swollen by the back water from the harbour. The boy was carried out of his depth, and becoming exhausted with the intense cold, he sank. Fortunately a number of men were passing to the football match on the Athletic ground, and Richard Goodwin, a plasterer living in Furnace Lane, seeing the lad's danger, went into the water and brought him out. The boy's clothes were put on, and he was hurried away home.

7 January 1913 Liverpool Journal of Commerce
Bishop of Liverpool's Tribute
Chief Engineer's Heroism

If there was one man who truly deserved a fitting recognition of heroic work in the terrible *Titanic* disaster, it was the Chief Engineer, Mr Joseph Bell. It was generally considered that the engineering staff of the *Titanic* was the cream of the fleet, and that amongst these Mr Bell stood out as a noble and stalwart figure. Under such circumstances, last night's ceremony of unveiling a tablet to his memory at St Faith's Church, Crosby, by the Lord Bishop of Liverpool, was happily appropriate. Mr Bell was a native of Maryport, Cumberland, where he was born in March 1861. He served his apprenticeship with Messrs. Stephens and Co. Newcastle-on-Tyne, and after a brief period of employment with Messrs. Lamport and Holt, he joined the White Star Line as the sixth officer on the old *Adriatic* in May 1887. By January of 1891 he had worked himself up to the position of chief engineer of the *Coptic,* and subsequently held that position on a number of the White Star Line's steamers, being for a time the chief of the *Olympic,* and finally that of the *Titanic*. The late Mr Bell held a First Class Senior Engineer's certificate in the RNR, and was a man of the finest and most endearing characteristics....a very handsome cut stone tablet was set up by the late chief engineer's widow. It bore the following inscription:

To the glory of God and in loving memory of my dear husband Joseph Bell, chief engineer of the 'SS Titanic', who was lost with all his engineering staff in the foundering of that vessel after collision with an iceberg in the Atlantic Ocean, April 15th 1912. Faithful unto death...

Perhaps what had impressed the public most was the dauntless heroism of the brave men who, deep in the very bowels of the ship, worked the engines until they could work them no more. And one of those was the gallant chief engineer to whose memory that tablet was dedicated.

18 April 1913 Whitby Gazette
A Salt Of The Old School

The death of Captain Benjamin Nelson, Harbourmaster of Maryport, which occurred at his home, Wood Street, Maryport, on Monday, last week at the age of seventy-two years, has removed a salt of the old school, who, in sailing ship days, had many stirring adventures. On one occasion, when commanding a British ship in mid-Atlantic, he saved the entire crew of a Norwegian barque which had become a total wreck. The men were taken off at night, in bad weather, and for his seamanship, the late King Oscar of Norway presented him with a handsome telescope suitably inscribed.

9 October 1913 SS Volturno

At about 6 in the morning of 9 October 1913, the *SS Volturno,* a liner carrying passengers, many of them immigrants, from Rotterdam to New York, caught fire in mid-Atlantic. There was a gale blowing at the time; one of the cargo holds exploded and soon the ship was engulfed in flames. The fire soon spread to the ship's coal bunkers, and cut the power to the pumps. Nonetheless, the crew fought the fire for another two hours before realising that it was not possible to stop it. Captain Inch radioed an SOS, which was answered by eleven ships, one of them being the *Devonian* whose First Officer was Tom Steele, from Maryport. The rescue ships formed a ring round the stricken vessel, to try to cut off the effects of the huge seas, then launched boats to take off the passengers. It was almost impossible to take the boats alongside the blazing ship, for fear of being smashed against her side. Seeing that the passengers were reluctant to jump into the freezing waters, Chief Officer Steele and his volunteer crew took their boat right alongside the *Volturno* and took off a number of passengers. Having succeeded, they approached the vessel twice more, and took off a total of sixty-three passengers. This was the first boat to approach the blazing ship. Seeing the success of this boat, the boats from other ships were encouraged to follow suit. In all they save five hundred and twenty-one passengers and crew. One hundred and thirty-five people died.

For his courageous actions in taking his boat alongside the *Volturno* when no-one else was willing to do so, Chief Officer Steele was honoured by the British and Belgian governments. He received the Albert Medal from King George V at Buckingham Palace, The Lloyd's Medal for saving life at sea, the medal of the Life-Saving and Benevolent Society of New York, and the Liverpool Shipwreck and Humane Society, for bravery at sea.

Captain Steele had not given up serving his country, joining the Home Guard in the Second World War. He collapsed and died shortly after finishing his duty patrol with the Maryport Home Guard, aged 65, in 1941.

7 July 1914 Runcorn Guardian

Prince, a black retriever owned by Mrs Duggan, of Irish Street, Maryport, has been awarded the Bronze Medal of the Canine Defence League for saving a four year old child from drowning at Maryport.

Prince was a curly haired dog belonging to Mrs Duggan, who was a widow. A little girl fell into the River Ellen and there were no adults about. She would have drowned if Prince had not jumped in, grabbed the back of her frock in his teeth, and dragged her back to shore.

1914-1918 Maryport Medals for Bravery

The Victoria Cross is given "For Valour".
The Distinguished Service Order was for "gallantry in the field" given to Captains and above.
The Distinguished Service Cross was given to officers for "distinguished conduct before the enemy".
The Distinguished Conduct Medal was given to other ranks for "distinguished conduct before the enemy.'
The Military Cross was given to officers "For Bravery in the Field".
The Military Medal was given to other ranks 'For Bravery in the field".

Where details have not been discovered, the name of the person winning the medal has simply been recorded.

Lieutenant Eric Pearson Adair, RE. Military Cross

When he enlisted, Lt. Adair lived in Maryport. At the time of his award, his parents, Mr and Mrs Louis Adair, had moved the family home from Selby Terrace, Maryport, to Allonby. Lieutenant Adair was made an Associate Member of the Institute of Civil Engineers just before he enlisted.

According to the Wigton Advertiser, 20 April 1918, Adair's daring soon saw him promoted to Captain. In 1918 he was severely wounded whilst the engineers were fighting as infantry. He was hit by a rifle bullet in the thigh. A sapper gave him first aid, but soon the order came to evacuate the trench and retreat. The troops moved out until Adair and the sapper were last. The sapper took Adair on his shoulders, piggy-back style and set off to carry him out. The Germans were 100 yards from them and bullets were flying round. Captain Adair was hit again, this time in his other leg. He was now quite incapable of gripping his rescuer with his legs. He said "I'm done. Put me down in a shell hole and go on and save yourself." The sapper refused and hoisted Adair onto his shoulders, staggering on. They came across two more walking wounded also retreating and the sapper attempted to help them. Then he picked up Adair again and struggled onwards, carrying an 11 stone man for one and a half miles over heavy ploughed ground to the new British front line trench.

Sergeant Alex Aitkins RFA   DCM

Petty Officer RG Baxter RN   DSM

Cpt. Richard Baxter S Staffs Regt. Military Cross
   Captain Richard Baxter was the son of Mr and Mrs Robert Baxter of Curzon Street, Maryport. He was the son of Mr and Mrs Robert Baxter, and was a teacher at the Maryport County School on the outbreak of war in 1914. In due time, he obtained a commission and distinguished himself in very heavy fighting, which resulted in him being awarded the MC for his

gallantry and resourcefulness in leadership. He was twenty-five in 1918 and had married Miss Jefferson, from Holme Cultram.

In April 1918 he was reported as missing, but this seems to have been because his name was confused with that of another officer of the same name in the same regiment.

John Benson RGA   Military Medal
Gunner Benson was listed as having won his MM during the great advance of August-September 1918.

Sergeant J Black RFA   Military Medal
Gunner Sgt. Black was gazetted his MM on 19 February 1917

Lt. Percy Broatch Border Regt.   Military Cross
Percy Broatch was promoted to Temporary Second Lieutenant and posted to the Northumberland Fusiliers. He received a Military Cross for conspicuous gallantry and devotion to duty. He led his men into an attack and got onto action on his final objective in a very short time. Half of his men became casualties, but he still kept his mortars firing and supplied with action until he was relieved after three days of fighting. It was because of his brilliant leadership and cheerful example that the mortars fired during that time and kept the enemy back.

Sergeant J Brough DLA   Military Medal

Brough, of the 20th Bttn. Durham Light Infantry, was gazetted his MM on 23 July 1919.

Lieutenant W Brown   DSC

Private W Buckley Border Regt.   Military Medal

Gazetted 4 February 1918.

Sergeant D Clark ASC   Military Medal

Douglas Clark was a famous rugby player and wrestler, and when the First World War broke out, he was at the peak of his abilities. Of course, he volunteered to join the army. In 1917 he was out in No Man's Land during the battle of Passchendaele, collecting the bodies of wounded comrades, whilst under fire, when a shell exploded near him. He sustained eighteen shrapnel wounds and spent weeks in hospital, finally being discharged in a wheelchair. In just under four months he was back in the front line with his comrades. He was gassed at Passchendaele, and again on his return to the front but returned to high level sport after the war.

A modest man, and a great sporting hero, he is buried in Maryport Cemetery; the letters 'MM' for his bravery in the war, do not appear on his headstone.

Dr Frank W Clark   Military Cross

Frank Clark was the son of Dr RL Clark and lived at number 2 Fleming Place.

William Clark

He served in the Royal Field Artillery throughout the Great War, and latterly as a dispatch rider. He won his Military Medal for outstanding bravery under enemy fire. After the war he ran a successful butcher's business in Maryport.

Corporal Robert Douglas   Military Medal
Died of wounds 6 November 1918.

William Elliott RFA   Military Medal

Leading Seaman John Ferguson RN   DSM
He was gazetted in the Distinguished Service Medal on 12 October 1918 for his courage during the Zeebrugge raid of 23 April 1918.

David Graham Seaforth Highlanders   Military Medal

Private Graham was from Flimby and was gazetted with the Military Medal on 25 May 1918, probably for courage in resisting the great German offensives taking place from March to August of that year. He was apparently presented with a gold watch.

Gunner G Graham   Russian Medal
Gunner Graham was presented with the Russian Medal of St George, 4th Class on 4 August 1917. He was an acting bombardier at the time.

Lance Sergeant JC Graham EYR   Military Medal

Graham, of the East Yorkshire Regt. was awarded his medal in September 1918 during the great advance that ended the war.

Rev James Wharrier Hall   Military Medal

The Reverend Hall, formerly a curate in Maryport, was a stretcher bearer in France, was gassed twice, and taken prisoner, then held in a POW camp in Germany. He died aged 46 in 1932, never having fully recovered from the gassing.

Private RW Hodgson, Lanc. Fus.   Military Medal

Before the war, Mr Hodgson was a boy messenger at Maryport Post Office, before going to Workington as a postman. He was awarded his medal in the 1918 New Year's Honours List for something he did in November 1917, possibly at Passchendaele or Cambrai. In 1944 he was appointed Postmaster at Peel, on the Isle of Man.

Private J Jackson Border Regt.   Military Medal

Jackson was gazetted of his MM in January 1918.

Capt. Herbert Johnson Welsh Regt. Military Cross

Captain Johnson was a sniper, and was later appointed sniping instructor to the US Army. A one-time resident of Maryport, he had become acting manager of the Glengarw Colliery in Blaengarw. He was awarded the MC in January 1917.

Corporal F Kelly N Lancs   Card of Honour
So many acts of bravery were not rewarded with medals. In such cases, the commanding general of a division wrote a card informing the soldier that he was aware of what had been done, and commending his courage.

Private JM Kelly Royal Fusiliers   Military Medal
Kelley's medal was gazetted on 27 July 1918.

Corporal TH Lee   DCM
Lee won his medal in action in December 1916. He came home wounded and was decorated in January 1917.

Private JW Little Border Regiment Military Medal
On Thursday 28 March 1918, at the Cooperative Hall in Maryport, Private JW Little was presented with £50 and a gold watch and chain by his fellow members of The National Federation of Blast Furnacemen (Cumberland and Lancashire District), and his employers The Workington Iron Company. This was to mark his achievement in winning the Military Medal. It was gained by a display of gallantry and devotion to duty in rescuing wounded comrades under fire in a fierce battle. Private Little was subsequently discharged because of wounds, and

went back to his old employment at the Solway Ironworks. Mrs Little was also presented with a handsome gold locket and chain.

Captain NS Millican Liverpool Regt. Military Cross

Norman S Millican was the son of a well known Maryport sea captain, JW Millican. He received the Military Cross for exceptional services in France during the final stages of the battle of the Somme in 1916 where he was wounded. By January 1917 he was convalescing at home in Maryport before returning to the front. About 10.30pm on 29 July 1918 he was out in No Man's Land, in very faint light, when a hun sentry in a listening post hit him with a shot which went clean through his left breast and, coming out under the shoulder blade, wounded a private in the shoulder. He was taken back to the Endsleigh Palace Hospital in London, where he had been treated for his first wound. The specialist who examined him said that he had had the luckiest escape imaginable.

Sergeant Major F Melville   Croix de Guerre

Sergeant Major Melville was from Maryport, and had been in the Cumberland and Westmorland Police, being stationed at Penrith, Whitehaven and Maryport. His brother, by 1917 was an Inspector based in Penrith. Before the war he left and went to live in Canada but when war broke out, he joined the Canadian Dragoons and served in France where he was severely wounded. He then returned to action once recovered. The French government awarded him the Croix de Guerre, announced in July 1917, for exceptionally gallant conduct during a reconnaissance patrol. Shortly after this, he was mentioned in despatches, again for gallantry.

Private J Menhams   Military Medal

Menhams evidently won his Military Medal in the closing stages of the war, being presented with his medal in August 1919.

Sergeant R Messenger   Military Medal

Bombardier JE Metcalf   Military Medal

He worked in Maryport Co-op and won his medal on 2 November 1918, just nine days before the end of the war.

Lance Corporal John Mulgrew RE   Military Medal

Mulgrew was a Pioneer in the Royal Engineers. His award appeared in the Gazette in February 1917.

Stoker John Palmer RN   DSM

Stoker Palmer worked in the Maryport Co-op. On 23 April 1918 Palmer was a stoker on board *HMS Intrepid*. This old light cruiser had been selected to be one of the block-ships to be sunk and deny the Germans the use of Zeebrugge for their U Boats. She was filled with concrete, along with *HMS Thetis* and

HMS Iphigenia and steered by a skeleton crew into the entrance to the Bruges Canal. The ships were under heavy enemy fire as the Germans concentrated on trying to stop them. Of about 1700 men in the attack, 227 were killed, 377 wounded and 19 taken prisoner. The volunteer crews of the block-ships had to make their escape by boat as best they could; this was one of the most daring operations of the war. Stoker Palmer, of 22 Fleming Street, was wounded in action.

Cpl. GG Perceval Northumberland Fus. Military Medal

Perceval's medal was awarded in July 1919.

Signaller Sergeant H Peters Border Regt. Military Medal

Peters was gazetted of his MM in January 1918.

Captain JD Proud RAMC - Military Cross and Bar

John Proud was the son of Dr Frederick Proud and his wife Jane, who lived at 12, then 18 Curzon Street. He studied medicine from 1910 to 1915 before being commissioned into the Royal Army Medical Corps as a lieutenant. His Military Cross came as a result of working for forty-eight hours under heavy fire on the battlefield, and bringing in many severely wounded men whilst in charge of a team of stretcher bearers. Later he worked a continuous five days, virtually with no rest, directing his bearers and tending wounded men under fire, with conspicuous gallantry and devotion to duty. For this he was awarded a bar to his Military Cross.

On 28 July 1918 he was wounded while directing his bearers and bringing in the wounded of an infantry brigade which was in the process of an attack. He died of wounds on 1 August 1918, his colonel writing of him, 'He was quite fearless, and one of the best officers I have ever had serving under me.'

In the Medical Gazette, a former colleague wrote, 'It was with the greatest regret that I heard of the death of JD Proud, and I am sure all who knew him will mourn the loss of one of the best men who ever attended our college of medicine. He was a capital fellow in every way, being a good and keen student, a good sportsman, and, above all, a good comrade, always willing to give you a helping hand if in difficulties. I saw JD just about a month before his death, and little did I think it would be the last time, because he was so bright and cheery. It is a great pity he has paid the supreme price, because he had done so well in the army, having attained the rank of captain in the RAMC and having gained the Military Cross with bar for valour in the field. In conclusion I will say I am exceedingly sorry this war has deprived us of such a pal and has deprived the medical profession of such a promising member. A friend.'

Lance Corporal W Reay RE   Military Medal

Commander Maurice Regan RNVR   OBE

Maurice Regan was a Naval Transport Officer based in Hull, and in 1917 he was a Lieutenant. He was employed by Mathwin and Co., coal suppliers to the fleet, then joined the navy in the same capacity. He was one of the first OBEs, being gazetted on 7 January 1918 in the New Year's Honours list. The citation gives no clue as to what he had done save that it was awarded for services connected with the war.

Private J Rudge Northumberland Fus.   Military Medal

Joseph Rudge's award was announced on 3 September 1919. He was from Grasslot, Maryport and was in the Ministry of Munitions Hospital, at Gretna where he died in 1920. It is possible that he was carried off by the great flu epidemic of that winter.

Lance Corporal Matthew Simpson Military Medal

Simpson was in the Labour Corps and was gazetted his MM in January 1919, though it was announced in September 1918 during the Great Advance.

Sergeant Edward Smith   VC

Ned Smith was born in 1899, and at the age of fourteen was employed at Oughterside Colliery, and also joined the Army Reserve in 1915. He must have faked his age, because in 1916 he enlisted in the Army, and by December was serving in France with the 1/5 Battalion Lancashire Fusiliers. At this time soldiers were supposed to be eighteen to join up. and nineteen before they could be sent to fight abroad. Young he might have been, but Ned had found his niche in life, and was so good at soldiering that by August 1918 he had been promoted to Sergeant.

During the great advance of 1918, nineteen-year-old Sergeant Smith took command of a platoon which was held up by an enemy machine gun post. He attacked the enemy post himself, armed with a rifle and bayonet, utterly disregarding the hand grenades that the enemy lobbed at him. Reaching the German position he killed at least six Germans and took their position. For this he won the Distinguished Conduct Medal. Shortly afterwards he saw that a neighbouring platoon was in difficulty, so he led his own men to their relief, and both platoons then attacked and took the enemy position.

The DCM is only awarded for outstanding acts of bravery.

The German counter-attack on the next day, succeeded in pushing part of the British line back, so Sergeant Smith took forward one section and recaptured what the Germans had taken.

For his bravery, skill and initiative, he was awarded the Victoria Cross, the UK's highest award for bravery, on which are inscribed two simple words "For Valour." Smith was the youngest winner of the VC in the Great War.

Edward Smith VC

When Smith returned home to Maryport, six thousand people turned out to cheer him when he arrived; the whole population of the town was no more than this. Visiting his old colliery, he was presented with a gold watch and Albert, whilst his mother received a cameo brooch, and his father a new pipe. The town of Maryport presented him with £141 in war bonds, and he had a further £30 4s from the local coal conciliation board, along with a new clock for his home.

Smith's father was a Maryport seaman who served with the Royal Naval Reserve at the Dardanelles and Gallipoli. His brother, in the Royal Field Artillery, was wounded twice in action.

After the war, he stayed in the army, serving in China, Malaya, and Ireland, rising to the rank of Regimental Sergeant Major before retiring in 1938. For about a year he joined the Corps of Commissionaires, but then came war. He rejoined the colours as a lieutenant and was killed in action by a gunshot to the head, fighting the Germans on 1 January 1940 near Buquoy, France. He is buried in Beuvry Communal Cemetery extension, Nord Pas-de-Calais.

It would seem that courage ran in Smith's family. His grandfather was for many years Coxswain of the Maryport Lifeboat and saved many lives. He was known as 'lion-hearted Benn,' for his courage in the worst of seas.

Lance Corporal M Smith   Military Medal
Lance Corporal Smith was an employee of the Maryport Co-op. He won the Military Medal for gallantry on the field, and devotion to duty. A committee of the company presented him with a gold watch , Albert, and pendant as a token of their esteem in November 1918.

Private JW Stansfield DLI   Military Medal

Stansfield, from Maryport, was a teacher at Crook School, County Durham, and enlisted in the Durham Light Infantry.

Private TW Stansfield   Military Medal

Stansfield was from Maryport but had emigrated to New Zealand. He came back to fight, and was awarded his medal in New Zealand.

Bombardier Percy Studholme CFA Military Medal

Percy Studholme was the eldest son of Mr J Studholme, Station Master at Maryport. Formerly a railway clerk, he had gone to live in Canada in 1911. When the war began he joined the Canadian Field Artillery. He won his Military Medal on 6 November 1917 when the Canadians attacked and took the Passchendaele ridge.

Sergeant William Studholme RFC   Military Medal

Sergeant Studholme was the second son of Mr J Studholme, Station Master at Maryport, and was a railway clerk in the office there. He joined the army in 1915 at the age of 18-and-a-half. During the autumn of 1917 he was awarded the Military Medal for his part in shooting down an enemy aircraft, under daring circumstances. He then went home on leave, but a few days after returning to the front, he was again involved in aerial combat. During the fighting he received wounds and injuries which proved fatal.

Joseph Thompson RFA   Military Cross

This was a posthumous award. Captain Thompson was killed in action on 26 October during the Great Advance. He was from Maryport, then Allonby.

Reginald Todd   Military Medal

Reg Todd was and apprentice engineer on the Maryport and Carlisle Railway who attested at the age of 15. When 18 he joined the army, and became a hero at age 19. Under heavy fire, during an engagement with the enemy, he carried wounded men of the Black Watch from off the battlefield and to the aid stations. Mr Hartley, Chairman of the railway company, presented him with a gold watch as a mark of his colleague's esteem.

Lance Corporal L Trainer Border Regt. Bar to MM

Trainer was gazetted with a bar to his Military Medal in August 1918 during the great advance. His original award was gazetted in March 1917.

Private D Turner Border Regt.   Military Medal

Sergeant Urwin RFA   Mentioned in Despatches

Driver David Watson RFA   Military Medal

Driver Watson, of the 11th Royal Field Artillery was from Maryport, but lived in Blackpool, and it was from there that he enlisted. In March 1916 he wrote to the Blackpool Gazette and Herald, asking the people of Blackpool to send socks and gloves as the men were experiencing the worst of weather, snow and frost, and terribly cold winds. He won his Military Medal in November 1917.

Private J Wedgewood Border Regt. Military Medal

John Wedgewood died on 30 July 1916 while his regiment were taking part in the battle of the Ancre, a part of the larger Battle of the Somme. The regiment were digging advanced trenches for future operations when they came under shellfire and gas. Private Wedgewood was killed in action. Private Wedgewood, of 8 Bttn Border Regt. was killed while attending to wounded under very heavy shellfire near Souchez on April 17th 1916.

Gunner N White RFA   Mentioned in Despatches

Gunner White was promoted to Bombardier on 18 September 1917, and his bravery mentioned in despatches.

Lt. H Wild (NF)   Military Cross

Lieutenant Wild was killed in action on 21 August 1918 and is buried at Bucquoy on the Arras-Amiens road. His regiment was the Northumberland Fusiliers, though he was attached to the Lincolnshire Regiment at the time of his death.

Private W Young RAMC   Distinguished Conduct Medal

22 June 1918 Whitehaven Advertiser and Cleator Moor and Egremont Observer
Honouring a Maryport Hero

A letter was read from Mr RB Fearon, Secretary of the Committee which is organising a testimonial to Private W Young RAMC who has been awarded the DCM, stating that Mrs Senhouse agreed to make the presentation, and asking the Chairman to be present and support her.

The Chairman said the Council could not subscribe without the consent of the Local Government Board.

Mr Hadry moved they ask the townspeople to subscribe and to do something handsome indeed for Pvt. Young.

The Chairman had great pleasure in seconding. Of course it did not go for anything unless they saw that others subscribed, and without subscribing themselves, they could not tell others to subscribe. (Laughter)

Supplement to *the Gazette* April 1918

Private Young of Maryport, was awarded his DCM 'For conspicuous gallantry and devotion to duty. As medical orderly attached to a tank battalion, though blown up and wounded, he performed his duties with the utmost coolness, attending to infantry wounded cases as well as those of his own battalion. He accomplished fine work in helping to extinguish the burning clothing of two men. Throughout, he displayed the greatest devotion to duty and an entire disregard of personal safety.'

Private Young actually won his medal on 23 November 1917 during the battle of Cambrai. He was tasked to follow the tanks towards the village of Fontaine and tend to the Tank Corps wounded. He was thus *ahead of the advancing infantry.* The infantry never reached the village, as determined German resistance stopped the advance. Young tended infantry wounded as well, in the very heart of the battle.

THE 1920s

27 May 1921 Yorkshire Post and Leeds Intelligencer

An inquest was held at Maryport yesterday on Miles Swinburne, who was found drowned in a disused pit shaft. Swinburne being missed, the shaft was first dragged, but without avail. Then a sailor named McNellon and a miner named Hodgson descended the shaft which was 40ft deep and full of foul atmosphere. From an improvised raft, they dragged the water in the shaft with a line, to which were attached fishermen's skate hooks. These caught in Swinburne's clothing and brought him to the surface. The Coroner, in returning a verdict of "found drowned", warmly commended the pluck of McNellon and Hodgson.

31 May 1922 The Lancashire Daily Post
Gallant Rescue at Maryport

John Mulgrew, collier, Scott's Yard, Nelson Street, Maryport, effected a gallant rescue yesterday. A child of three, son of William Burns, collier, Nelson Street, fell into Maryport Harbour when the tide was full. Mulgrew, who was near, flung off his coat and plunged in, diving a distance of about ten feet from the quay into the water, narrowly missing a fishing boat in his descent. He secured the child who was hauled up onto the quay. The boy was little the worse for his immersion.

13 November 1923 The Lancashire Daily Post Maryport Boy's Plucky Rescue of Dog

William Armstrong (13) a schoolboy living in Nelson Street, Maryport, and son of Mr J Temple Armstrong, an old Maryport Rugby footballer, was the hero of a gallant episode yesterday. A Labrador retriever had fallen into Maryport Harbour, and although a powerful swimmer, was rapidly becoming exhausted.

Young Armstrong volunteered to try to rescue it. A rope was fastened to his body, and he was let down the quay to the dog. The boy displayed great presence of mind and nerve. He secured a foothold on a narrow ledge, unloosened the rope from his body and fastened it to the dog, which was hauled up. The rope was again lowered and Armstrong was hauled up to safety.

26 March 1925 Western Morning News

Miss Jennie Stoddart and two men were highly commended by the coroner at an inquest at Maryport yesterday for their heroic conduct in entering a burning house and trying to save an old lady.

Mrs Mary Harrison, a blind nonagenarian, was sitting in her armchair when the fire broke out, and, though bravely rescued, she died a few hours later. She could not walk without assistance, but she had crawled along the floor and signalled with her hand from the window for assistance.

24 August 1925 Staffordshire Sentinel
Omnibus Wrecked

A 14 seater omnibus, owned and driven by Lowery Nixon, of Dearham, running full into Maryport on Saturday night, when rounding a bend at Netherton, in avoiding a motor-cycle, crashed into the garden wall of Carswell House. The vehicle was overturned and wrecked.

The passengers, mainly women, displayed great courage and coolness. All suffered from shock, and were more or less injured, some requiring medical attention.

25 September 1925 Lancashire Evening Post
Maryport Youth's Bravery Rewarded

At the Town Hall, Maryport yesterday, the Royal Humane Society's Vellum was presented to Henry Hodgson (19) Fleming Street, and Robert Kirkbride (20) 82 Nelson Street, for bravery displayed on the afternoon of Sunday 24th June, when Robert Hine (13) was drowned. Hine, who was bathing with other boys from the South Shore, was carried by the flowing tide round the end of South Pier into the channel. Hodgson divested himself of his coat and vest while a girl, who was standing near, loosed his boots. He then scrambled down the end of the pier, a difficult and dangerous task, and entered the water. Hodgson, who is by no means an expert swimmer, was some time in finding the boy, who had been washed some distance along the channel and towards the North Bank. At length however, he got hold of the body and put it over his shoulder, when Kirkbride, who entered the water from the North Bank, came to his assistance, and the body was conveyed to the North Bank where artificial respiration was tried, without success. When in the water, he found his trousers weighing him down and he managed to kick them off.

The Maryport Amateur Swimming Club took the matter up and Mr JJ Routledge collected the sum of £15 as a damaged clothing compensation fund. Five pounds of this was given to the lads £2.10s each, and the rest kept in reserve for future cases.

The presentation last night was made by Mr G Ferguson, Chairman of the Urban Council, Dr Sanderson, chairman of the swimming club presiding.

5 October 1925 Lancashire Evening Post

The Royal Humane Society has awarded a parchment to John Osmotherley (23) fireman, 4 Brown's Yard, Eaglesfield Street, Maryport.

15 October 1927 Eckington, Woodhouse and Staveley Express

This newspaper carried an article about the death of Mr WH Ball who was, for seven years, manager of the Flimby and Broughton Moor Colliery at Maryport. During his stay at Maryport, he displayed conspicuous bravery at an explosion in the St Helen's Colliery when he and two other men saved many lives. In commemoration of this heroic act he received a beautiful silver salver as a lasting sign of appreciation from the St Helens Colliery and Brickworks Company

Ltd. It recorded his valuable services in the fire in the Main Band on Jan. 7th 1904.

20 December 1927 Penrith Observer

The Royal Humane Society awarded its recognition on vellum to William Donachy, 23, dock labourer of Maryport, who, on October 30th, saved John Banks, aged 13, who had fallen into the water of the harbour.

7 January 1928 Liverpool Journal of Commerce

Captain W Frodsom was born at Maryport on 15 November 1857, and in May, 1874, when 17 years of age, he ran away to sea in the brig 'Uranus', which was lying in Maryport Docks. After a round trip of nine months he returned home to Maryport, and his parents, realising a strong desire to follow a sea career, recommended that he be apprenticed to a firm of sailing ship owners. This, however, was not to the liking of young Frodsom, for in December, 1877, he again cleared off to sea on his own...(some years elapsed).

On passing for Master, Captain Frodsom made several short voyages, and in March 1886 he entered the service of the Lamport and Holt line. In 1889, while he was second mate of the Lamport and Holt Belgian mail steamer 'Helvelius', the ship broke down in the Bay of Biscay. The sea was too heavy to launch lifeboats, and, the vessel being in great danger,

Captain Frodsom swam in a boiling sea with a line to the steamer 'Loughborough,' which was standing by the 'Helvelius', but was unable to effect a communication. By means of this line, hawsers were passed between the two vessels and the 'Helvelius' was eventually towed into Ferrol. For these services, Captain Frodsom received a gold watch from his company...

Captain Frodsom's first command in the Lamport and Holt Company was in 1899 when he was appointed to the steamer 'Herschel', which was the second ship of that name owned by the company. When in command of the 'Terence' in 1917, that vessel was attacked by a German submarine, at one o'clock in the afternoon, when she was 100 miles west of the coast of Ireland. A strong defence was put up by the vessel against the German submarine, and at six o'clock the same night the 'Terence' was attacked by three submarines, and after a hard fight of five hours against such overwhelming odds the ship was torpedoed, as in the darkness the gunners and those on the 'Terence's' bridge were unable to manoeuvre so as to avoid the oncoming torpedoes. Captain Frodsom and his officers and crew took to the boats, and after five days they reached the Irish coast.

In recognition of his gallant services on that occasion, Captain Frodsom was awarded the DSC, and received a letter from the Lords Commissioners of the Admiralty, expressing their opinion that the greatest credit was due to him for his courage and fine example which he set on the occasion of the attack by three submarines upon the 'Terence'.

On the 15th October 1918, the Liverpool and London War Risks Insurance Association sent Captain Frodsom a special resolution of thanks for the seamanlike skill and courage shown by him on the occasion of the determined attack made upon his vessel the 'Herschel' on the 1st October 1918, and voted him 100 guineas out of the funds of the association as a mark of their appreciation.

Captain Frodsom was subsequently appointed to the command of the new 'Herschel', which was the third steamer of that name belonging to that company. She also was attacked three times by enemy submarines, one torpedo passing under the bridge, but, fortunately the vessel herself sustained no damage. While in the 'Herschel' Captain Frodsom was successful in picking up 70 men, forming the crew of the Greek steamer 'Ioamina', which had been torpedoed off the western islands.

After the war he commanded several steamers of the line, the last being the steamer Hogarth from which he retired at the end of the year. He takes with him into his retirement the best wishes of the directors and officials of the Lamport and Holt line, as well as of his many colleagues in the Merchant Service.

13 November 1928 The Penrith Observer
Night Fire Rescue at Maryport
Family's Ordeal above Burning Shop

A family of six living above a Maryport grocer's shop which caught fire late on Monday night were rescued only with great difficulty. The father, after being rescued by neighbour, went back into the burning house and rescued three of his children. He was then exhausted and neighbours rescued his wife and baby, the wife having to jump from an upper window into a blanket. The outbreak was discovered at 11.30. Neighbours burst open the door, and the proprietor, James McMullen, was assisted to escape. But when he realised that his wife and family were still inside the house, he rushed back through the smoke and flames that had driven back the neighbours. He was the only one who knew where the children slept, and he made three separate entries, bringing a child out with him each time. He was too exhausted to do more. A man named Minchella then went inside to rescue the baby, but he fell, overpowered by the smoke.

Thereupon an ex-serviceman, named James Poland, ascended to a bedroom by means of a (human) ladder entered the house, and seized the baby from a bed which was already in flames. In doing so he was badly scorched. He appeared again at the window and dropped the baby down to those waiting below. He then went back to help Mrs McMullen. He assisted her into a bedroom on the second storey, and from there she jumped into a blanket held by neighbours below. At first she hesitated to jump, as she did not know her youngest child had been rescued. Another neighbour, James Cullen also showed great courage in assisting the work of rescue. Both Mr and Mrs McKullen were severely injured, and others were less seriously hurt. The premises were burned out and when the fire brigade were fighting the flames, a floor collapsed under Captain Longcake and he, and several others, were injured.

On Thursday 28 December 1928, the Carnegie Hero Fund Trustees awarded memorial certificates for bravery to Robert Kirkbride of 87 Nelson Street, Joseph Poland of 107 Nelson Street, Louis Minchella of 13 Marshall's Place, and James Cullen of 100 Nelson Street, all of Maryport. Whether James or Joseph, the press seemed unable to decide, but the hero of the fire lived at 107 Nelson Street, and that is plain enough. The ladder that Mr Poland climbed up was made of three men; Messrs. Minchella, Cullen and Kirkbride. At the ceremony there came a dramatic moment when Mr Minchella's former sergeant major rose and testified to Mr Minchella's great courage at the battle of the Somme where he fought in the Lonsdale Battalion.

THE 1930s

6 April 1931 Shields Daily News
Fully Clothed Man's Dive to Save Boy

William Scott, a pit-pony driver, who a few years ago represented the Council School, Maryport, in a swimming team race at Maryport Regatta, rescued a three year old boy named Shilton, who, on Saturday, fell from the Quay into Maryport Harbour when the tide was flowing full.

An alarm was raised, and Scott, fully clothed, plunged ten feet into the water. Grasping the drowning boy, he swam to some steps, which enabled him to carry him to safety.

In July 1931 William Scott attended at Maryport Council where he was presented with the Royal Humane Society's certificate for saving life, on parchment, for saving the life of Tom Shilton, of King Street. He was also presented with a sum of money. Mr Scott worked at the St Helen's Colliery.

6 June 1931 The Wigton Advertiser

Percy Jones, aged 17 of High Street, Maryport, a newsboy, rescued a nine year old boy, William Smith, of George Street Maryport, from drowning in the River Ellen. The child was playing on the bank of the river when he overbalanced and fell in. Jones jumped in after him and got him out none the worse for his ducking. This is the second rescue Jones has effected on the same spot.

21 July 1931 Lancashire Evening Post
Honour for a Maryport Boy Hero

At Maryport Council meeting last night, William Scott, formerly a pit pony driver at St Helen's Colliery, was presented with the parchment certificate of the Royal Humane Socety and a sum of money, for saving the life of a four year old boy, son of Tom Shilton, King Street, Maryport, on Good Friday. Scott was on the quay and heard a cry. He saw a boy in the water and plunged, fully clothed, from the quay into the harbour, making a ten foot dive. He reached the child and swam with him to some steps in the quay wall.

The Chairman, Mr Nathan Friend, in handing over the parchment and money, said Scott was a credit to his parents, to his town and to his country. Had it not been for Scott's heroic conduct, the child would have been drowned. He hoped he would live many years to treasure the parchment and show it to his friends.

20 October 1931 The Daily Mail

John Yeomans, an unemployed miner, of Nelson Street, Maryport, ran 200 yards along the Maryport Quayside and made a 30 foot dive, fully clothed, into the harbour, and rescued a six years old boy named Binn, of the North Quay, Maryport. The boy had fallen into the water while at play.

29 June 1932 The Yorkshire Post
Maryport Youth makes his Fourth Rescue from Drowning

Tom Dixon, aged seventeen, who is employed at Siddick Colliery, Maryport, made his fourth rescue from drowning yesterday. Norah Gilmour, a child of four years, fell from some steps at the North Pier into the sea. She had ceased to struggle and was floating head submerged when Dixon saw her.

He sprinted 30 yards, plunged in, and brought her out. The child recovered after first aid treatment.

8 June 1933 The Lancashire Daily Post
Rescue Drama off Maryport Pier
Battle with Current

Prompt help from the shore averted what might otherwise have been a tragedy on Maryport dock shore last evening.

Alice and Nellie Cartmer, sisters of High Street Maryport, aged 21 and 19 had been for a long swim with Joseph Graham of Grasslot, Maryport. Both girls are good swimmers and Graham is a strong swimmer, but when they returned they found the current which swirls round the end of Maryport Pier, and runs straight out into Allonby Bay, running very strongly.

Nellie battled through, Graham accompanying her until she was comparatively safe, and then returned to Alice. By this time Alice had drifted considerably nearer the pier where the current increases in strength.

Graham got to her and got her to put one hand on his shoulder, but even with the girl helping and Graham using his full strength, time passed and they had not gained an inch on the current. Eventually Graham was compelled to shout for help.

Andrew Nixon, Catherine Street, Maryport, heard him, shouted to Jim Nixon, his son, on the shore, who went in dressed except for shoes and jacket. On reaching Graham, he took the girl and decided to try

with the current for the pier. He succeeded, and Graham, relieved of the extra duty, was able to make the pier himself, though all three were dangerously near to the end when they got a grip and were able to scramble on two of the wooden pier beams.

16 January 1934 The Wreck of the *Plawsworth* Bravery at Sea

The morning of 17 January 1934 was wet and stormy, a gale blowing all the night, and it would not reach its height until the afternoon. AE Jolly, the mechanic of the Maryport Lifeboat had gone down to the boathouse and with his second, had cleaned the spark plugs of the engine, and then given it a test run. Just about a quarter past eleven, they had finished and went to go home for lunch. Coming across a group of men he knew, including the bowman of the lifeboat, Jolly stopped to chat. One of the remarks passed among the men was that they would not be surprised if they got a call-out that day; if they did, it would be the worst weather they had ever been out in.

After a few minutes, Jolly went on his way, but he never reached his lunch. Down the High Street he came to Coxswain Thomas Reay's house, just as he came dashing out, waved his hand at Jolly and shouted "Owwer". As they ran, Reay gasped out that a steamship had run aground near Workington. There were some men already at the lifeboat station when they got there, and the maroons were fired, exploding over the town with a deafening "Crack", alerting the

rest of the crew to drop what they were doing and come running. Within five minutes, rollers had been laid out to carry the boat across the road and onto the slipway. The mast was up, the engine was started; the rest of the crew piled onto the boat and pulled on life-jackets, and the head-launcher let the cable go. Down the slipway the boat slid, and into the water, heading out of the harbour and into the teeth of a 60mph gale. The engine of the boat would not make much headway against such a wind, sometimes gusting to 70mph, and the boat hoisted its sail, tacking and using the south-westerly to make headway as the engine was not powerful enough to fight the wind on its own.

Visibility was bad, and even when the spray cleared from their faces, the lashing wind belted it into their eyes again, men shouting 'It washes the eyes right out of me'. The only person who had an eye-shield, made of mica, was the coxswain, and even he could not see much because of the constant stream of water down his vision. The wind was so strong anyway that it flattened the shield against his face.

The seas were huge, and when the boat was about a mile off shore, between Seaton Scar and Siddick pit, it was plunging into troughs so deep that all the crew could see were walls of water fore and aft. For each dive the boat took, the helmsman kept her head to the waves, and she rose up the next wave as steeply as if going up the Fells. The boat was thirty-five feet and six inches long, and each wave slope that they sailed up was two-and-a-half times that. Small wonder that some of the men felt sea-sick and had to shake it off somehow and tend to their duties.

All seven men were now soaked to the skin as the water found its way down the sleeves and necks of their oilskins. Perhaps the wettest was the bowman who stood at the very front of the boat, holding onto the mast to steady himself, facing the oncoming fury of the waves, and keeping a sharp lookout for the ship they are going to help. Immediately behind him were two extra volunteers, both fishermen, for whom this was the first time out in the boat. They sit waiting and may not be needed, for they are there to pull the oars if necessary; for the moment the oars stay stowed away. As the waves washed over the boat, they were repeatedly waist-deep in freezing water. Behind them were the first and second mechanics, and finally the coxswain and his second; the coxswain mans the wheel, which struggles so much that he has to jam his whole body between the spokes to keep the boat on course.

The crew were tired now; constant buffeting by wind and water slamming at them made them feel like punch-drunk boxers as the cold soaked into them; but now the bowman shouted out that he could see the wreck. Fresh energy poured into the crew's muscles; here was danger and they were needed; lives had to be saved. At this time the wreck was so far away that her people could not be seen. The lifeboat was a mile off-shore, and now the helm was turned towards the wreck to allow the wind to assist in the approach; the lifeboat's engine could now be used to manoeuvre her.

The lifeboat came down to the wreck, which was the *SS Plawsworth* starboard to starboard, about fifty yards away from her, the wreck being stern on to the shore. They were now so close to the shore that they could see Siddick slag banks and the men onshore with life-saving equipment. That side was impossible, so the lifeboat turned and battled round the ship to the port side. The first wave that came along as they rounded the ship, took them away towards the shore, towards the rocks, but she struggled off. Inch by inch she crept seaward along the ship's side, approaching the stern where it was expected that the crew would come off.

The wreck signalled that the crew would come off near the bow; the stricken ship was split in two, and her plates were open above the waterline. The lifeboat's engine was going flat out to maintain her position, but inch by inch she managed to claw her way out to sea, ahead of the wreck. The coxswain ordered that an anchor be dropped, meaning to allow the boat to be carried down to the ship where the men could be taken off, but the bowman paid out the anchor and it did not hold.

Once again the boat was swept landward and had to claw her way off at full engine. This time, with a sharp note in his voice, the coxswain ordered the anchor to be *dropped,* not paid out. It held.

Now the coxswain ordered that the engine be switched to idle, and the waves carried the lifeboat down towards the wreck as they paid out the anchor rope. The lifeboat was thrown about like a cork until they were ten feet from the bow of the steamer, where the crew had gathered, all wearing lifebelts. A rope had been thrown to link the wreck to the lifeboat. The coxswain shouted at the waiting men not to rush things but to come one at a time; he was trying to adjust the position of the boat, constantly calling out orders to Mr Jolly; "Ahead!", "Stop", "Astern!". He simply could not place the lifeboat where he wished so that the waiting men could jump down onto her, and the rope joining the two vessels kept on snapping. One of the crew did jump but missed his footing and ended up half in and half out of the lifeboat, having to be hauled in bodily.

When the rope joining the vessels snapped for the second time, the lifeboat was thrown hard against the sheer side of the steamer, damaging her steering gear. At least the lifeboat was hard up against the wreck now, and the crew began to jump for their lives. Ten or twelve made the leap until one was left, an elderly man of about fifty. He was hanging on to the ship's rail, about to jump, when the coxswain shouted 'Not yet!' He stayed clinging, and the warning was justified, for the lifeboat was swept further towards the shore, and he would have jumped into the sea. It took some hard work for the engine and a few minutes before they could get the lifeboat back into position.

When they got to where they wished to be, the boat was rising and falling so savagely that the elderly man had to wait, clinging on in the wind and wet, until the coxswain shouted 'Now!' and he jumped. He landed right on the second mechanic, so had a good soft landing.

The *Plawsworth* was being battered by the sea, and though her anchors were out, they were still dragging; the very thing that had set her on the rocks in the first place. The lifeboat was on the port side, but the wreck was slowly turning to starboard, so that the rescuers were more and more exposed to the raging seas. No more of the wreck's crew came to jump, but two men in gold and silver caps appeared and shouted to the lifeboat.

'That's the lot; the rest are staying for the present.'

The coxswain replied, 'How many?'

'Five'.

'Sure you won't come?'

'Yes. Thank you.'

Now the coxswain gave the order to cast off the rope connecting the lifeboat to the ship, and the men heaved on the anchor cable, pulling them out towards the sea and away from the wreck. Now Jolly put the engine to full throttle. Inch by inch she clawed her way out to sea, only just making any way at all.

The rescued men were very grateful to be off the wreck, and there were many thanks, one man giving the coxswain half a pound of shag tobacco as a gift, though it was socked with sea water. The *Plawsworth* had endured eight days of gales, and had dropped anchor off Workington the previous night. A huge wave hit her which knocked her steering gear out of action, and dragged her anchors so that she ran backwards onto the rocks. Her plates had burst, some of her holds were full of water, and the ship had split so that the after-deck was moving under their feet, which was why they had all moved forward.

The lifeboat's steering gear was jammed in the starboard position, but the coxswain managed to coax her out to sea far enough so that he could turn and make a good run into Workington Harbour which they reached some fifteen to twenty minutes after leaving the wreck. As they sailed up the calm harbour waters, many people appeared and cheered them to the place where they moored and set thirteen rescued men ashore. Within a few minutes the damaged yoke of the steering gear was unbolted and being repaired by a local marine blacksmith. It did not take long because just as it was being fitted back into position a man shouted that the lifeboat was needed again, back at the wreck.

The lifeboat once again headed out into the gale and bore down towards the wreck. It was now impossible to get to her. She had turned broadside onto the rocks and was heeling over onto them so steeply that her side was high out of the water on an ebb tide. Nothing could be done, so the lifeboat returned to Workington where the coxswain was told that the *Plawsworth* would be high and dry in an hour when the tide had receded enough. The men on board would be able to walk ashore.

The sea had not finished with the lifeboatmen however. As they headed back towards the harbour a huge wave curled over their stern and swept the boat, flooding it and almost broaching her. The men in the front were submerged, then slowly their heads and shoulders emerged; the boat was filled to the gunwales and the crew sat in water. The coxswain was quickly with the wheel and get the boat once more end on to the waves, while relieving valves took most of the water outboard. She must have been heavy though, because she did not let the next wave pass under her. Instead she rose on top of the wave which carried her along like a surfer and at great speed. As luck had it, they were carried in exhilarating style, several hundred yards towards Maryport. By the time they reached Maryport Harbour, there was still sufficient water over the bar to enter, and they did so to the cheers of a crowd that had been waiting to greet them home.

Coxswain Thomas Q Reay of Maryport, received the RNLI Bronze Medal for saving life at sea.

Mr AE Jolly, who was not a seaman, but a mechanic, received the RNLI scroll on vellum for saving life at sea. Each member of the crew received £2 8s 6d

15 May 1934 The Lancashire Daily Post
Maryport Rescue
Boy falls over Bridge 30 feet into River

Robert Reeve, an eight year old boy residing with his parents at Coronation Street Maryport, had a narrow escape from drowning in the River Ellen when he fell from the bridge into the river in the middle of New Road.

The boy had been with his parents to his grandfather's home in Senhouse Street. On his parents leaving, he had turned back to his grandfather's home, and had then set off to follow his parents.

How he came to fall over the parapet of the bridge is not known. The boy was knocked unconscious by the force of the fall into the water from a height of approximately 30 feet, and was floating down the river when a woman passing raised the alarm.

He had floated a considerable distance before the attention of two young men was attracted, and they pulled him out of the water near the sewage pipe which crosses the river from the end of Mill Street.

22 August 1934 The Lancashire Daily Post
Maryport Rescues
Men save two Boys and a Father his Son

Maryport Harbour was the scene of three rescues within the space of two hours yesterday. Eric Nixon, Crosby Street, and another schoolboy, named

105

Henderson, of Queen Street, were fishing near the harbour when Nixon fell in. Henderson, in trying to help, also went in. Neither could swim.

Charles Scholey, a young man of King Street saw the boys in the water shouting for help and went in for them. James Scott, another King Street man was quickly on the scene and followed Scholey immediately, just as Councillor W Graham was preparing to go in from the Grasslot side.

Between them, Scholey and Scott got the boys out, both subsequently recovering completely.

About two hours afterwards, John Brown, aged 10, of South Quay, Maryport, ventured down a ladder to try to retrieve a ball for a little girl. He fell into the water off the steps. However his father noticed what had happened and promptly climbed down into a rowing boat into which he pulled the boy.

Curiously, the third boy, John Brown, is a cousin of James Scott, the rescuer in the first instance.

6 August 1934 The Lancashire Daily Post
Maryport Hero
Young Man's Seventh Rescue of Drowning People

A whistle was nearly the cause of a drowning tragedy at Maryport on Saturday evening. William Moore, aged 4 years, of Strand Street Maryport, whilst playing with a whistle on the steps of the north quay of the harbour, lost the toy, and, in endeavouring to retrieve it, fell into the water.

John Yeomans, a young married man, of Nelson Street, Maryport, immediately threw off his jacket and took a header off the top of the quay, quickly bringing out the boy who was tightly grasping the whistle. The boy recovered after attention.

This is the seventh occasion on which Yeomans has played the principal part in rescues from drowning at Maryport in the course of the last few years.

18 December 1934 Yorkshire Post and Leeds Intelligencer
Boy's bravery rewarded

William James Hamilton (16) of Maryport, Cumberland, was presented at Maryport Town Council meeting yesterday, with a certificate for bravery. Two Maryport boys fell into Maryport Harbour, and Hamilton plunged in, and held both until help arrived.

19 December 1934 Lancashire Evening Post

Mr John McCullough, who died at the Black Lion Inn, Maryport, was awarded a certificate and medal by the French Minister of Marine for the part he played in rescuing the crew of a French ship during the war. At the time Mr McCullough was serving in the Mercantile Marine. He was 76 and is survived by his wife and two daughters.

6 April 1935 The Lancashire Daily Post
Maryport Fire Rescue Drama
Neighbour Saves Family

A fire broke our early this morning in a shop with a dwelling house above, in Nelson Street, Maryport. Hearing a woman screaming "Fire," James Poland, a neighbour and seaman, dashed out half-dressed and in his stocking feet.

He kicked open the door of the shop and found two children named Hindle, huddled on the stairs, which were thick with smoke, and carried them out.

Returning, he entered the first storey bedroom, and found William Parker, an elderly bedridden invalid, and asthmatical, in bed and unable to move, with one side of the room on fire and the bedclothes beginning to blaze.

Poland carried Parker out on his back. Mrs Parker and her widowed daughter, Mrs Hindle, got out safely.

Neighbours came in night attire and formed a bucket chain until the brigade arrived and quelled the fire.

13 July 1935 The Lancashire Daily Post
Fisherman's Dive into Harbour to Save Boy

James Elliot (19) a fisherman, of North Quay, Maryport, saved a lad named Banks, aged about eight, from drowning in Maryport Harbour yesterday. The boy was playing in a boat in the harbour when he fell into the water.

The tide was at its height, but Elliot ran to the harbour edge, and, fully clothed, plunged in and brought the lad to safety.

21 October 1935 Lancashire Evening Post

The Finnish steamer Esbo was thrown ashore in a gale at Bootle, South Cumberland on Friday 18 October. It appeared that her passengers and crew could not be saved by line to the shore, so the alert went out to the Maryport Lifeboat.

Lifeboat Crew's Bravery

Maryport lifeboat crew made a gallant bid to reach the *Esbo.* When the lifeboat was launched, it was hurled like a cork, broadside against the North Pier, and Coxswain TQ Reay almost washed overboard. It took expert seamanship to get the lifeboat back into harbour where it was necessary to overhaul it for damage, and also to lash coxswain Reay to the stanchion of the wheel. At the second attempt, the lifeboat got out to sea, and for four hours it battled its way towards the *Esbo,* and got to within 200 yards of it. The lifeboat crew saw that the ship was deserted, with every sign that the Whitehaven Rocket Brigade had been successful in taking off the crew. The return journey was almost as bad as that on the way out.

Motor mechanic Jolly said their cox was the hero of the day. "There was some shelter for the six of us in the boat, but Coxswain Reay was up, lashed to the wheel, taking the full force of sea and weather the whole time. But for the lashings he would have been gone a hundred times, and the boat and the rest of us with him, for all depends on his skill. Today he is suffering acutely. His right side is injured through being battered against the stanchion to which he was lashed, and his head is bruised. The weather has virtually closed one eye, and he is suffering considerably from exposure."

In recognition of Coxswain Reay's efforts, he received a framed letter of thanks from the RNLI Board, and £43.10s to be allocated to himself and the lifeboat crew.

30 November 1935 The Lancashire Daily Post "VC" for Maryport Dog

Rex, the five year old Bedlington terrier of Mr J Thompson, Ellengrove, Maryport, is to be Maryport's first "VC" dog.

Rex earned the distinction by the part he played in rescuing his young mistress Joyce Thompson from the River Ellen behind their home at Ellengrove in July, while Rex's kennel companion, a Great Dane, that could have whisked the child out of the water without any trouble, refused to enter the river, but ran up and down the bank barking approval at the terrier's efforts.

When the girl fell into the river, the terrier kept her afloat until Robert Johnstone, a young unemployed man arrived, and, although a non-swimmer, got the girl out.

16 March 1936 Yorkshire Post and Leeds Intelligencer
Unemployed Man's Eighth Rescue
Dived into Maryport Harbour to save Boy

William Johnston, a 24 year old unemployed man of Nelson Street Maryport, Cumberland, dived from a moored boat in Maryport Harbour on Saturday, and swam through icy water to rescue John Watson (6), son of Mr and Mrs TW Watson, 43 King Street Maryport.

The boy had fallen into the tidal harbour from the steps of the north quay, used by fishermen to get to their boats. His father stated that the boy had just returned from a sanatorium, following a bout of pneumonia, and was in delicate health. Johnston got to him just in time to save his life.

It is believed that this is the eighth time Johnston has rescued someone from the waters at Maryport, and he has yet to receive his first recognition. On Saturday he ruined his only suit in making the rescue and had to stay at home until his father could obtain some clothes from a friend.

8 October 1936 The Daily Mirror
Rescue Dive at 56

A fifty-six year old unemployed man ran 200 yards and dived fully clothed into the Elizabeth Dock, Maryport, Cumberland, yesterday, to rescue Margaret Edgar, aged five, of Grasslot, Maryport.

He was Thomas Miller, of Nelson Street, Maryport. Hearing cries for help, he ran to the dock, and though out of breath, he dived into the water. He was attacked by cramp, but succeeded in bringing the child to safety.

The girl is in a critical condition.

10 October 1936 Hartlepool Daily Mail

Alan Fisher (5) of Wells Lane Maryport, Cumberland. was rescued from drowning at the old shipyard, Maryport yesterday by another boy, James Mossop (16) of Crosby Street Maryport who dived into the water, and although carried 50 yards by a strong current, brought him to safety.

19 May 1937 The Lancashire Daily Post
Maryport Rescue Award

The Royal Humane Society's Certificate for Bravery, awarded to Robert G Aitcheson, a grocer's assistant, of High Street Maryport, was presented last night to the youth's father by Mr T Blair (Chairman) at the Maryport Urban District Council.

Mr Blair said that Aitcheson, who was away from Maryport and unable to attend the ceremony, was taking his first walk after influenza, last winter, and found a small boy had fallen off the north sea wall into the tide. Fully clothed, Aitcheson went into the water and rescued the boy.

29 July 1938 Edinburgh Evening News
Heroism for 7/6 Prize

It was marathon day yesterday at Glasson, Maryport, Cumberland, and the course lay over slag bank and seashore - mighty rough going.

Dick Peacock of Glasson, slimly built, 16-years-old lost his foothold near the top of 100ft high Glasson slag bank. Women in the crowd screamed as he fell from the path down an almost perpendicular drop of 70ft, in two somersaults, a bounce, and finally a 20ft slide.

Men ran to aid Dick. Picking himself up, he waved them aside, and with gashes on arms and legs, ran the remaining 300 yards to victory.

Women relatives had to be held back to allow him to finish.

Dick turned up in bandages later to receive his prize - value 7s 6d.

23 January 1939 The Scotsman

The Royal Humane Society has awarded Vellums to Wilfred Howard (13) 10 North Quay Street, Maryport, Cumberland, and Thomas Benn (13), 2 Tyson's Yard, Strand Street Maryport. The boys saved the life of Jack Montgomery, aged 5 of Wallace Lane, Maryport, who fell into Maryport Harbour on December 24 last, while watching some other boys playing marbles on the North Quay.

29 July 1939 Wigton Advertiser

Parchments of the Royal Humane Society, London, for bravery in life-saving, have just been issued to the following:

To Patrick Gray (55), a blast furnace man of 135 Senhouse Street, Maryport, for rescuing James Smith, aged 11 of 15 Grasslot Street, Maryport, who, on May 24th 1939, fell into the River Ellen at Maryport, having climbed outside the railings of the bridge.

THE 1940s

6 February 1940 The Lancashire Daily Post
Maryport Rescue Dive in Dark
Soldier's Gallant Act

Diving into Maryport Harbour in the dark, Private Stephen Richardson, of North Quay, Maryport, supported George Rogan (62) of Ewenrigg Cottages, Ellenborough, Maryport, for 15 minutes until both were rescued by a boat.

Mr Rogan lost his way in the black-out about 9.10pm on Sunday night, and walked over the quay not far from Christ Church. Private Richardson and Mrs Richardson, who had gone out to post a letter, heard his cries for help.

While Mrs Richardson struck matches to locate the edge of the quay, her husband threw off his outer clothing and dived 20 feet into the running tide. She then shouted for help and men who came along put out in a small boat, and picked up the two in the water. Her husband had supported Rogan for 15 minutes.

Both suffered from shock as a result of their immersion. Private Richardson suffered a bump on the head in diving, and is suffering from a severe cold. Mr Rogan was revived by St John's Ambulance men, and was also attended by a doctor.

Man fell, grasped boat

Earlier the same evening, Mr Fred McKeown of Strand Street, walked off the quay at a place not far away. As he fell into the harbour, he struck a small boat, moored near the side. Although a non-swimmer, he was able to grasp the boat and hang on until help came in answer to his cries.

19 October 1940 Lancashire Evening Post
Brave Maryport Youth

Seaman William Patterson (18) son of Mr and Mrs Patterson, of 9 Wallace Lane Maryport, has been commended by the Rear-Admiral in command of his flotilla for his prompt and courageous action in going overboard to the assistance of Stoker Nussey, off Iceland. It is understood the youth dived overboard to rescue the stoker.

2 November 1940 Cumberland News

Private, acting as Sergeant JS McLean of the Border Regiment, was awarded the Distinguished Conduct Medal. He was in 4 Company Border Regiment and was part of the British Expeditionary Force, being evacuated from France in 1940. John Somerville McLean was gazetted on 23 August 1940. Evidently a soldier of some merit, he made the leap from Private to Lieutenant, later being assigned to the Cameron Highlanders.

18 February 1941 Lancashire Evening Post

The Royal National Lifeboat Institution has awarded to Coxswain Thomas Q Reay, of Maryport, a clasp to the bronze medal which he already holds, its thanks, on vellum, to the motor mechanic Herbert Rook, and £2 17s 6d to the coxswain and each member of the crew for rescuing four men from the herring drifter *Mourne Lass,* of Workington, on a night in October last.

It was blowing a full gale, with fierce squalls and blinding rain. The drifter was helpless. Her nets had fouled her propeller and when the crew tried to sail her home, the wind split the mizzen sail to shreds.

When the lifeboat reached her, the crew had given up all hope of living through the night. *It was with the greatest difficulty that the exhausted men were got onto the lifeboat.*

It was a half hour back to Maryport Harbour in pitch blackness. There was no light onshore because of the wartime blackout. Coxswain Reay held a sure and firm course in very rough seas until he knew from his own experience, that he was close to home. He flashed his morse lamp towards the shore and was answered by the harbourmaster flashing his torch. With only that to guide him, he steered the lifeboat through turbulent waters and blinding rain into the narrow entrance to the harbour , bringing all safe ashore.

Thomas Reay retired from the Lifeboat Service in April 1942 after thirty-six years of service, ten as the coxswain. He won the Institution's Medal for Gallantry in saving life at sea, twice.

14 June 1941 Lancashire Evening Post
MM for Maryport Soldier

Signaller Christopher Moore of the Royal Artillery has been awarded the Military Medal. He is the first Maryport man to gain an Army decoration in the present war.

The only news received by his mother, Mrs Poland, of Brooklands Avenue, Maryport, is that he received the award for gallantry in action at Gallabat on the Sudan-Eritrea border, last November.

He was wounded in the fight, and was in hospital for some months afterwards. Aged 23, he has served for five years in the Middle East.

16 August 1941 Cumberland News

Harry Birkett was the Chief Engineer on board the 'SS Anselm'. The ship was torpedoed and Birkett survived eighteen days in an open boat.

On the morning of 5 July 1941 U96 fired a salvo of four torpedoes at 'HMS Cathay', an armed merchant cruiser and the British survey vessel 'HMS Challenger'. They missed, and two hit the troopship 'Anselm' instead. She sank in twenty minutes; four crew members were lost and two hundred and sixty service personnel. The corvettes 'Starwort', 'Petunia' and 'Lavender' then attacked the U96 and damaged her so severely that she had to abort her patrol and return to base.

In the confusion Harry Birkett was missed, having drifted out of the combat area, until he was picked up, dehydrated and starved, eighteen days after the sinking.

1 April 1942 Liverpool Echo
'Snow for Christmas'
Courage of a Wounded British Seaman

Picture a British able seaman on the deck of a stricken and sinking ship, his right foot blown away, and the leg just above it shattered. Then read his reply to his mother, sent from a German prison camp as to how he came to survive with such injuries, a reply only sent after many requests:

"I was in the water three hours. I have my lifebelt away when I was hit, but I was alright with a small bit of wood under my arm, for I am not a bad swimmer. The chap I gave my lifebelt to was saved. He is a non-swimmer so he was pretty lucky."

The writer is Able Seaman Cuthell, 29 years old son of Mr and Mrs A Cuthell, Grasslot, Maryport,

Cumberland. He was transferred to the navy with his ship, *HMS Voltaire.*

"We had snow for Christmas" he says, "the only thing we had extra except a parcel from the British Red Cross."

20 November 1942 Lancashire Guardian

PC Matthew Crayston, a native of Burton, has retired on a medical certificate from the Cumberland and Westmorland Constabulary after serving the last 23 years. When quite a youth he joined the Army in September 1914, his regiment being the 8th Borders (Kendal Pals). He won the Military Medal and later, a bar, receiving also a special leave from France for good patrol work between the lines. Before his 20th birthday, he attained the rank of Company Sergeant Major, and was wounded at Passchendaele in 1917. His police activities since the Great War include periods at Workington, Whitehaven, Keswick, Penrith, Cleator Moor, Harrington, and Maryport for the last five years.

28 November 1942 Cumberland News

Joseph Dawson of Maryport, Chief Officer of the Blue Star Line *Empire Star* was awarded the OBE for conspicuous gallant service relating to the fall of Singapore.

By 11 February 1942 a British defeat at Singapore was probably inevitable. The *Empire Star* loaded with close to two thousand people, left Singapore as part of the evacuation convoy.

It was not many hours before she was attacked by six Japanese dive bombers; one was shot down, and another damaged, but three bombs hit the *Empire Star*. Fourteen people were killed, including the second officer. She was on fire in three places, but her fire fighting equipment was still functional. Chief Officer Dawson organised fire-fighting parties that extinguished all three fires and saved the ship. The *London Gazette* recorded his conduct as follows.

"The chief officer showed great organising ability and tireless leadership throughout."

9 January 1943 Cumberland News

Leading Gunner T H Lee, of Ellenborough, Maryport, was awarded the Distinguished Service Medal for his actions in Arctic Waters.

6 February 1943 Newcastle Journal

Flight Lieutenant Maurice Williamson of Maryport, Cumberland, has been awarded the DFC, it is announced. In June last year this officer was detailed to attack an enemy installation. His aircraft was attacked by a Junkers 88 and suffered severe damage. By skilful manoeuvring, Flight Lieutenant Williamson

Flight Lieutenant Williamson

flew the aircraft back to base. In September, while attacking enemy shipping at Tobruk, intense enemy anti-aircraft fire was encountered, but he pressed home his attack with considerable success. "This officer" says the citation "displayed conspicuous gallantry throughout his operational career, and his devotion to duty has been outstanding."

16 October 1943 Cumberland News

Flying Officer John James Pattinson of the Royal Air Force Volunteer Reserve was awarded the

Distinguished Flying Cross for high courage and devotion to duty. In the 1946 New Year's Honours List he was named as a Flight Lieutenant and mentioned in despatches.

1 January 1944 The London Gazette

Petty Officer Robert Fisher, RNR LT/X 7353 Maryport, Cumberland, was mentioned in despatches in the New Year's Honours List.

4 March 1944 Lancashire Evening Post

News has reached Mr and Mrs Cuthell, Solway Cottage, Grasslot, Maryport, that their third son, William Cuthell RAMC, has won the Military Medal serving in Italy. Cuthell was originally in the RASC in France, and was at Dunkirk. He has two brothers serving - one having been repatriated from Germany, and a third has been in the Army.

8 June 1944 Liverpool Daily Post

Petty Officer William Reay, Maryport, was awarded the British Empire Medal (Military).

27 November 1944

At 1838 hours, a de Havilland Mosquito, of 109 Squadron RAF, took off from RAF Little Staughton, near Bedford, for a bombing raid against Neuss in Germany. The pilot was Flight Lieutenant Maurice Williamson (RAFVR) and the navigator was Flying Officer Albert Kitchen (RAFVR). Over the Ijsselmeer in the Netherlands, the Mosquito encountered heavy flak. Despite this, it was not enemy action that brought it down, but engine failure and it had to be abandoned, a very hazardous procedure. F/O Kitchen was killed, his body being found later, and F/Lt. Williamson baled out, and was taken prisoner. Williamson already held the Distinguished Flying Cross which he earned in September 1941, but for his actions this day, he earned a bar.

Maurice Williamson came from Maryport, where, after the war, he was a prominent businessman. He lived in Christian Street. His parents were newsagents in Wood Street, and whilst he was a prisoner of war, his wife gave birth to their first child, a girl, at Maryport Hospital.

31 January 1945

Gunner Stanley Albert Roast, of Maryport, attached to number 1 Commando was stationed in the foremost weapons pit of his unit near Kangaw, Burma. His position was being constantly rushed and grenaded by determined Japanese troops.

He was firing a Bren gun, and his number two was wounded and unable to continue. Two other men who came to act as number two were killed and wounded. Gunner Roast did not retreat but continued to fire at the enemy, despite being alone on a forward slope with a Japanese machine gun firing at him from twenty yards away. He only left his position when the battle was won and he was relieved; in his time at his post he had fired over seventy magazines at the enemy. It was largely due to him that his unit's position was not over-run. For this he received the Military Medal.

17 April 1945 Yorkshire Post and Leeds Intelligencer

The Distinguished Flying Medal was announced as being awarded to Flight Sergeant IOD Waters, who was born in Leeds, but whose home was in Maryport. The award was gazetted on this same day.

5 May 1945 Lancashire Evening Post

The late Captain TS Wilson, Royal Corps of Signals, has been awarded the MBE. His wife lives at Great Crosby, and his parents, Mr and Mrs TS Wilson, at the Promenade, Maryport.

General Alexander, writing in support of the award, for his work in Ortona, Italy, said "He succeeded in restoring ordered life for the civilians in this battered city, and engendered among them, a confidence in the Allied cause."

Captain Wilson received two presentations before he left the city for forward duties, in which he was killed. One was a clock with the inscription "Presented to Captain TS Wilson, Governor, by the population of Ortona. Memories!" The other was a wallet from the staff of the technical office.

19 May 1945 Surrey Advertiser
DFM for Surrey Man

Flt.-Sergt. William Morrison Farish, RAFVR, number 357 squadron, whose home is at Woking, has just been awarded the Distinguished Flying Medal. Born in 1923 at Maryport, Cumberland, he was a timber porter before enlisting in 1941, and was a member of the ATC number eleven squadron. As a wireless operator, states the citation, this airman has participated in numerous operational sorties. He has always been most efficient and thorough in his work, and has displayed exceptional keenness for operational flying, and great devotion to duty.

21 June 1945 Lancashire Evening Post

Mr Robert Leo Hine, of Kirkby House, Maryport, has been awarded the British Empire Medal for meritorious service in the Merchant Navy. He has served at sea throughout the war with the Eagle Oil and Shipping Company.

Until 1958 the BEM was often awarded for gallantry. That changed when the British Empire Gallantry Medal was instituted.

10 July 1945 Lancashire Evening Post

Leading seaman Robert Bowie, a native of Maryport, has been awarded the DSM for bravery, determination, and skill in operations against enemy submarines.

Leading seaman Bowie won a scholarship for Workington Technical and Secondary School, and finished his schooling at Carlisle Grammar School. Before the war he was employed in the LMS goods and passenger office at Carlisle. His brother, Corporal A Bowie, RAF, was recently mentioned in despatches.

27 September 1945 Lancashire Evening Post
George Medal for Maryport Sergeant

Sergt. George Hooper, youngest son of the late Mr and Mrs Hooper, Bank Lane, Nelson Street, Maryport, has been awarded the George Medal. In January last, a Flying Fortress crashed into a hangar in the mist on a Brussels airfield, and burst into flames. Sergt. Hooper, and Lieutenant Alan Cox, ran to the rescue, got into the hangar and found there were four airmen trapped in the burning machine. It was surrounded by pools of blazing petrol, and ammunition was exploding and firing in all directions. They got out one man each and dragged them to safety, then returned for the other two, but found the heat too intense. At that moment one of the rescued men raised the warning "Bombs!" The lieutenant and sergeant ran for safety and had gained 70 yards before they were blown flat by the bombs exploding. Lieut. Cox was also awarded the George Medal.

The George Medal was instituted in 1940 largely to recognise acts of civilian bravery, but also for acts where bravery was shown, not in a combat situation. It is given for 'Acts of Great Bravery' and ranks next to the Victoria Cross.

14 January 1946 Leicester Daily Mercury
Mine Immobilised

The fuse of a 1200lb British mine, which rocked at the end of a hawser ten yards from the sea wall at Maryport, Cumberland, all day yesterday, was removed by a Liverpool mine disposal squad late last night.

Three men volunteered to continue working at the gas-works nearby to ensure that Sunday dinners should not go uncooked. Forty families were evacuated from their homes, and NFS tenders stood by in case of fires should the mine have exploded.

26 July 1946 Uxbridge & W Drayton Gazette

An exciting day in the lives of a Yiewsley family was Tuesday, when they visited Buckingham Palace and ex-Sergeant Major John Hodgson, REME, of 2 Poplar Avenue, Yiewsley, was decorated by His Majesty the King with the George Medal for conspicuous gallantry at Calais.

The King asked Sergeant Major Hodgson of the incident that concerned the saving of a woman who was trapped in a cellar after RAF bombing. She was held fast by an iron bedstead, and the only method of release was an acetylene blow-lamp.

The CO in charge would not order this because of escaping gas, but Sergeant Major Hodgson took a chance, and after two hours the woman was released.

Mr Hodgson came to Yiewsley some sixteen years ago, and is a native of Maryport, Cumberland...

Maryport: home of heroes.

Finis

Printed in Great Britain
by Amazon

44988407R00076